DEADLY

DEADLY

DEREK UNDERWOOD
THE LIFE OF AN ENGLISH INTERNATIONAL CRICKETER

MARK PEEL

pitch

First published by Pitch Publishing, 2025

1

pitch

Pitch Publishing
9 Donnington Park,
85 Birdham Road,
Chichester, West Sussex,
PO20 7AJ

www.pitchpublishing.co.uk
info@pitchpublishing.co.uk

A CIP catalogue record is available for this book
from the British Library.

ISBN 978 1 80150 733 2

Typesetting and origination by Pitch Publishing

FSC
MIX
Paper | Supporting
responsible forestry
FSC® C016779

Printed and bound on FSC® certified paper in line with
our continuing commitment to ethical business practices,
sustainability and the environment.

Printed and bound in India by Replika Press Pvt. Ltd.

Contents

Introduction

FEW IMAGES better convey the career of Derek Underwood than the one of him leading the successful appeal against Australia's John Inverarity in the fifth Test at the Oval in August 1968, the final wicket that gave England a famous last-gasp victory. In a series in which rain had twice saved Australia from likely defeat, the elements seemed destined to come to their aid once again when a cloudburst at lunchtime on the last day left the ground saturated. As the Australians, reeling at 85/5, celebrated in their dressing room and the England team cursed their misfortune, captain Colin Cowdrey was the one man who believed that all hope was not lost. Prevailing upon the crowd to help the groundstaff mop up paid dividends because by 4.45pm they were playing again.

With only 75 minutes left and a sodden pitch to bowl on, the England bowlers made little impression on the batsmen Inverarity and Barry Jarman, until the latter played on to a harmless delivery from Basil D'Oliveira. Cowdrey now switched Underwood to the Pavilion End and immediately he struck gold, dismissing Ashley Mallett and Graham McKenzie in one over as they lunged at lifting deliveries.

With the whole side clustered around the bat the tension was immense as the minutes ticked by. At 5.48pm, 12 minutes before the statutory close, leg-spinner John Gleeson was bowled by Underwood, and the BBC interrupted its transmission of the early evening news (then scheduled at 5.45pm) to return to the Oval. Cheered on by the nation from their sitting rooms, Underwood continued to pound the Australian defences and with six minutes remaining Inverarity, who'd batted throughout the innings, padded up to his arm ball and was palpably lbw. Amid scenes of euphoria, Underwood's 7-50 had enabled England to square the series and earned him a special place in Ashes history. Throughout his stellar career no performance gave him greater pleasure or so ingrained him in the national consciousness.

Born in Bromley on 8 June 1945, a birthday he shared with his future England captain Ray Illingworth, Underwood was raised in a loving middle-class home that revolved around cricket. His father, Leslie, was a useful village bowler and the net he installed in their garden enabled him to learn his craft. Bowling for hour after hour at his elder brother Keith, he developed his pinpoint accuracy and soon he became the talk of the neighbourhood as he made fools of men and boys alike. Attending Surrey nets at Croydon he was recommended to Kent by England spinner Tony Lock, and once on their books he was carefully nurtured by coach Claude Lewis, manager Les Ames and captain Colin Cowdrey.

Marking his first-team debut in 1963, aged 17, with 4-40 against county champions Yorkshire, Underwood continued to mesmerise batsmen with his unique brand of slow-medium left-arm spin, so that by the end of the summer he'd taken 100 wickets, the youngest bowler ever to accomplish this feat in his debut season.

The following year he won his county cap and in 1966, the year in which he topped the national bowling averages with 157 wickets, he made his England debut against the West Indies. Although success eluded him, he continued to flourish in the County Championship, especially on rain-affected pitches, where his prodigious turn and lift made him close to unplayable. It was only a matter of time before he replicated this success at Test level and following a promising summer against Australia in 1968, he came of age at the Oval.

A polite, self-effacing personality who behaved impeccably both on and off the field, Underwood was popular wherever he went. In an age when gamesmanship and sledging (verbal abuse) became more commonplace, he didn't insult his opponents or remonstrate with umpires. Describing him as one of the game's natural gentlemen, Sunil Gavaskar, India's legendary opening batsman, recalling his reaction to Gundappa Viswanath's century at Delhi in 1981/82, wrote, 'Who can forget Underwood applauding the exquisite century scored by Viswanath with a warm handshake and then saying to him, "Master, when you have had enough, please give your wicket to this bowler."' In Underwood's estimation, success was the cause for private satisfaction rather than public bombast and failure a challenge that needed to be surmounted. In the Kent tradition, where players and supporters formed a special bond, Underwood was the soul of humility, conversing with spectators, signing autographs and promoting the game at the grass roots. Even in retirement with over 2,000 wickets to his name, he was more content encouraging the players of the future rather than harking back to past glories.

Yet beneath the decorous charm and self-effacing temperament there lay a hard-headed professional whose competitive juices flowed as freely as any Yorkshireman. According to his England team-mate Geoff Boycott, he had 'the face of a choirboy, the demeanour of a civil servant and the ruthlessness of a rat catcher'. Whether it be a Test match or a benefit game, he hated conceding runs and on the few occasions he bowled a bad ball he would grimace in self-recrimination. A perfectionist like his illustrious team-mate Alan Knott, a wicketkeeper for the ages, he viewed any departure from the highest of standards as a lapse that needed immediate rectifying. Yet while stringent in his self-criticism he took exception to some of the armchair pundits who claimed he bowled too quickly or described him simply as a bad-wicket bowler. It is one of the paradoxes of his career that when the International Cricket Council (ICC) retrospective rankings rated him the world's leading bowler between 1969 and 1973 he was in and out of the England side during that time, omitted normally for Norman Gifford, Worcestershire's slow left-arm spinner. While there may have been something in captain Ray Illingworth's contention that in favourable batting conditions Underwood lacked Gifford's flight and spin, the records show that Gifford, fine bowler that he was, couldn't hold a candle to Underwood. And even when he wasn't among the wickets himself, he could take them for the bowler at the other end by stifling batsmen with his relentless control.

Underwood's other gripe concerned the reaction to his signing for Kerry Packer's unauthorised World Series Cricket (WSC) in 1977, along with England colleagues Tony Greig, Alan Knott, Dennis Amiss, John Snow and Bob Woolmer. In an age when trade union power had significantly raised the standard of living of British workers, the average pay for first-class cricketers lagged some way behind them. Still beholden to the Corinthian ideal that the game was played for love rather than money, the game's governing bodies ignored the lack of financial security that affected all players. Even allowing for the generous tax-free benefits that could accrue to seasoned professionals such as Underwood, top cricketers were poorly remunerated compared to other sportsmen.

Consequently, when Packer approached them, he found he was knocking at an open door. With a wife and family to support and with no obvious career to fall back on in retirement given his lack of qualifications, Underwood placed his loyalty to England to one side and signed. He knew it would attract controversy but the level of animosity, not least from some of his fellow professionals, left him aghast. The cruellest blow of all came the following year when the Kent committee terminated his contract and that of his Packer team-mates, charging him with disloyalty to the club he'd served with dedication for 15 years. Opposed by former secretary-manager Les Ames and a sizeable section of the membership, the committee later relented, but the hurt remained.

He continued to serve Kent with distinction for another decade and England for another 12 Tests in the post-Packer era, but he was never quite the same bowler again. Although he publicly expressed no remorse about joining WSC, he later regretted the loss of Test wickets. (He finished with 297.)

In time the benefits of the Packer revolution, not least the introduction of day-night cricket and the better remuneration for all sportsmen, helped rehabilitate the reputation of those who signed for WSC. More contentious was Underwood's participation in the 1982 England rebel tour of South Africa, then under sporting sanctions due to its apartheid regime, a decision that ended his Test career. It says much for his continued popularity that any resentment over South Africa didn't last and his standing in the game was fully recognised by his presidency of Kent in 2006 and MCC in 2008. When he finally succumbed to dementia in April 2024, the outpouring of grief told of a gentle giant whose relentless rise to the top never deviated from cricket's finest traditions. And that in essence is the central theme of this book.

Chapter 1

Beckenham Boy

DEREK LESLIE Underwood was born in Bromley Maternity Hospital on 8 June 1945, the younger son of Leslie Frank Underwood and Evelyn Annie Wells. The Underwoods hailed from the picturesque village of Yardley Hastings in southern Northamptonshire. Leslie's father, Frank Underwood, a constable in the Metropolitan Police, moved to Hampstead on his marriage to Annie Smith in 1907 and it was there that Leslie, born in 1914, was raised.

Derek's mother, Evelyn, was the only child of Arthur Wells and Annie Beddell, both from humble stock in Hertfordshire. A domestic gardener by trade, Arthur worked for the Bishop of Salisbury, and it was in the Wiltshire town of Devizes that Evelyn was born in 1913. Soon afterwards the family moved to the west London suburb of Hayes on Arthur's promotion to head gardener, and it was at Whitestone Pond on Hampstead Heath that Evelyn met Leslie. They married at Christ Church, Hampstead in 1937 and moved soon after to a semi-detached house in Daerwood Close, Bromley Common, then a village in Kent, to be closer to Leslie's place of work, Lane's Ltd of Bermondsey in south-east London. The company supplied air gun pellets, and as company secretary he was influential enough to be given a company car, a rarity in those days. Later, in 1955, by which time Leslie was managing director, the family moved again to the neighbouring village of Keston, and a new purpose-built home designed by an architect friend of Evelyn's, which they called Whitestone after the place where they had first met.

In what proved to be a very happy marriage – Derek's elder brother Keith was born on 5 July 1942 – Evelyn was the dominant force. While Leslie was gentle and charming, she was feistier and more opinionated, berating anyone who stepped out of line. Yet when not working hard to supplement the family income – she typed out legal documents at home for a company in London owned by Ray Cox, a task with which Derek, an accomplished typist, helped her – she devoted all her time to the family, catering for all their needs. Her preference for Derek contrasted with her mother Annie, who lived in the same road, for whenever he went to see her, she invariably greeted him with, 'Hello Derek, how's Keith?'

None of this favouritism disturbed the very close bond between the brothers from the time they shared a small bedroom together. In addition to collecting stamps, playing table tennis in the garage and fishing on Keston Ponds, both boys learned the piano and ballroom dancing at the school in Penge founded by Peggy Spencer, the doyenne of British ballroom dancing who taught Rudolf Nureyev, the greatest male ballet dancer of his generation, to tango. Yet all this activity paled into insignificance compared with cricket, their deep love of the game fostered by both parents. Leslie was a useful medium-paced bowler who played for his local village Farnborough every Saturday and Sunday. At an early age Keith and Derek used to watch him and play whenever they could, either in the road outside their house or on the beach close to their caravan at Whitstable. 'I remember that Derek could always get some turn with a tennis ball on the sand,' Leslie recalled. 'I used to make him bowl overarm from the start and he chose his left arm. He was very interested in the game, and I remember he used to pinch my big bat and go in the street to play.'

Hoping that his sons would represent Kent, Leslie laid down two concrete strips covered by matting in their large garden at Keston and put up some nets, so they didn't cause the neighbours any nuisance. There the two boys would practise for hours, Keith batting and Derek bowling. Being the only fielder and wanting to avoid endless sorties to retrieve the ball, he quickly learned the cardinal attributes of line and length which became such a feature of his career.

After both boys attended Princes Plain Primary School, Bromley, Leslie and Evelyn, appreciating that Derek lacked Keith's intellect, sent him to the elite Dulwich Preparatory School in 1954 to prepare him for 11 plus, the standard entry exam to grammar school. He remained academically limited but, ultimately, it didn't matter because Keith's progress at Beckenham and Penge Grammar School and Evelyn's membership of its Parent-Teacher Association there facilitated his entry without him taking the exam.

It is also possible that his prowess at cricket helped him, his 9-10 for the Dulwich under-10s the best of many spectacular returns. He owed much to the enthusiasm of sports master Mr T.F. Merritt, who used to take the boys to the Oval on a Wednesday afternoon to watch the great Surrey side of the 1950s. (He and Keith were also present when England regained the Ashes there in 1953.) In addition to greatly admiring the artistry of Peter May, one of England's finest batsmen, he loved watching Tony Lock, an orthodox slow left-armer with a quicker ball on turning pitches, to whom he was often compared in future although they possessed very different temperaments.

In 1958 Underwood enrolled at Beckenham and Penge Grammar School for Boys, founded in 1901 as Beckenham Technical Institute, before evolving into the above named in 1944 under the headmastership of L.W. 'Jumbo' White who retired in 1962, the year after Underwood left. The school, now Langley Park, a state academy, was highly prestigious and comfortably middle-class as working-class Bill Wyman, later a guitarist with the Rolling Stones, discovered when he was a pupil there in the early 1950s.

Underwood's future Kent team-mate Graham Johnson, a couple of years his junior, also attended the same school before moving to another one close by. He recalls first coming across him when the third form was forced to watch the finals of the school tennis to create atmosphere. He later relived the experience. 'Faced with the choice of supporting the school bully, who regularly stole our sticky buns at the morning milk break, my friends and I opted to support the other combatant who looked to have no hope as he basically seemed to be doing an impression of Charlie Chaplin on the tennis court, with the racket replacing the twirling walking stick. Sensing this gutsy, determined character could beat the hated bully we championed him and finding he responded to adoration and aided by the fact that the third form duces bribed the line judges, a close game ended with our man the victor.'

Underwood was a promising tennis player with the ability to switch the racket from one hand to the other to play forehand

and backhand shots, and he was also a useful hockey and rugby player. Yet whatever his interest in these sports they were a distant second to his cricket. Aged 14, he opened the bowling for the first XI with Keith, who was captain, and against Bromley Grammar School, the latter deliberately bowled wide of the stumps to enable Underwood to take all ten wickets. His gesture was typical of the loyalty that he always showed his younger brother, not least the great pride and pleasure he derived from his many future accomplishments. Underwood also scored 96 against the Masters, until he was adjudged lbw by the head of English.

When the brothers weren't playing at school they played for Farnborough under the captaincy of their father. In a side where the standard was mediocre, Keith recalled that not only were he and Underwood easily the best bowlers, but they were also the leading batsmen. Between them they bowled Deptford out for 9 and so humiliated were the opposition to be shown up by two schoolboys that they failed to stay for a drink after the game. Underwood also took 10-16 against Bromley Town and scored 45. 'Even in those days Derek used to set his own field and he always had these assets of accuracy and good length,' recounted his father.

To play at a higher standard Underwood joined Beckenham, one of the top clubs in Kent, in 1961 and there, under the supervision of former Kent cricketer Ronnie Bryan, he added variety to his bowling, producing a quicker and a slower ball. 'I used to bowl left-arm medium-fast,' he recalled. 'That was all very fine at school level. But when I moved up to the senior level, I found I had to develop something different.' Playing for Beckenham against Gore Court, Sittingbourne, the following year, the Underwood brothers took all ten wickets, inflicting on the home side their only defeat in their cricket week.

It was at Beckenham that he formed a lifelong friendship with Keith Patterson and his wife Erica and in 1962, attending the Bromley Town pre-season dinner with his father, he met another close friend, Martin Wigram, who recalls him as an ordinary teenager, intensely modest about his cricketing prowess.

During the winter Underwood's father took him to Allders indoor cricket school, situated in the basement of its department store in Croydon, for coaching with Surrey stalwarts Ken Barrington and Tony Lock. It was Lock who recommended him to Kent for his batting, an evaluation which manager Les Ames shared, but his assistants Claude Lewis and Colin Page spotted his potential as a bowler and advised him to make that his priority.

Lewis, who presided over the club's winter nets at Eltham, was a left-arm orthodox spinner who played for Kent in the 1930s, acting as an admirable foil to Doug Wright, the finest English leg-spinner of that era, and was nearing his peak when war intervened. Never quite the same player after the war, he became club coach, in which capacity he acted as a benign influence on the young for many years. According to Alan Knott, he was a kindly and dedicated coach while to Underwood, he was the most knowledgeable man in Kent following years of experience in the game. Lewis was really taken with Underwood's wonderful rhythm and action, later recalling that 'he was something unique in the way he fired the ball in at medium pace. I have never seen anyone like him.' Finding him to be a good listener, always willing to receive advice, especially the need to vary his pace according to the state of the pitch, he continued to be Underwood's trusted mentor and friend thereafter, not least when he became Kent scorer. During his later years when he needed the odd break Underwood thought nothing of standing in for him and using his coloured pens.

In 1960 Underwood represented Kent Schools, a side managed by George Pope, a genial schoolmaster who quickly detected his class and did everything to encourage it. Beaten only once in the previous five years, he preserved that record by bowling Kent Schools to a nine-wicket victory against London Schools with his quick left-arm cutters. Playing against him was Geoff Arnold, the future Surrey and England fast bowler. He later wrote, 'Derek soon impressed me with his bowling ability. Even in those days his accuracy and length were great assets, and one always felt that he would have a fine future ahead of him.'

Seven of that Kent Schools side were selected to play for the South of England Schools against the Midlands at Cranleigh, one of whom was the 14-year-old Knott. Very small for his age and wearing short trousers, he knocked on the dressing room door. When the manager saw him, he said, 'What do you want, son?' Knott replied that he was there to play. Born at Erith in south-east London, he was brought up in neighbouring Belvedere where his father was a pillar of the local cricket club. An accomplished wicketkeeper, he and his two sons played in the hall at home and in the street, the boys frequently hitting tennis balls into neighbouring gardens. Opening both the batting and bowling at school, Knott was taken to the Kent nets at Eltham, where he first came across Underwood. 'I think we were barely 12 when we first met and were still wanting to be fast bowlers,' recalled the former. 'I suppose back then we might have thought of having Underwood and Knott opening the Kent bowling.' Given his size, Knott was encouraged by Claude Lewis to switch to spin. Yet his agility behind the stumps, the legacy of his father's mentoring, had been noted and it was as wicketkeeper that he was selected for Kent Schools against the Midlands.

In a side that included Arnold, Peter Graves, the future Sussex batsman, and footballer David Sadler, later of Manchester United, Underwood stood out, taking 4-6. Standing back to him, Knott observed his nagging length and his slower ball which accounted for three of his four wickets. 'What was remarkable about Derek right from the outset was his accuracy,' he wrote. 'He so rarely strayed from his length and direction and could swing the ball in considerably to the right-hander.'

That following year Underwood was offered a trial by Kent, which meant surreptitiously missing the odd day of school because his headmaster disapproved of any disruption to his studies. Consequently, Kent batsman Arthur Phebey warned him to keep out of the sun, since a tan would undermine any excuse about ill health.

Selected for the Association of Kent Cricket Clubs (AKCC) juniors tour of the West Country in August, Underwood top-scored with 45 not out in their seven-wicket defeat by Sussex and took 3-32 in the draw against Dorset, then a week later, he took a hat-trick of lbws against Surrey at East Molesey. Playing in that team were Alan Ealham, who later became one of his closest friends, and Frank Ames, cousin of Les Ames, who recalls Underwood as pleasant but rather distant. He also marked his debut for the Kent Club and Ground with 5-19 against Metropolitan AKCC at Eltham, sharing the spoils with opening bowler John Dye, and for the second XI against Huntingdonshire.

At the meeting of the Kent cricket sub-committee on 24 July 1961, the minutes stated that 'The Manager was given authority to take on the Staff, D. Underwood, aged 16 years, and J. Dye, aged 18 years, both left-hand fast medium bowlers, at a weekly wage of £6.10.0d. for the former, and £8.10.0d. for the latter, plus £30 to £40 winter money.' On receiving the offer, Leslie Underwood, hoping that Derek's GCE results would be good enough to continue his education, wrote a non-committal reply to Les Ames, but when his exam results proved disappointing, he joined up in September.

Playing for the second XI against Hampshire at Beckenham in May 1962, Underwood was persuaded by captain Colin Page to bowl round the wicket because the ball was turning and he duly responded with figures of 5-45 and 4-15. The *Kentish Express* called his figures remarkable. 'The big question is, can he continue to turn in such figures?' it wrote. The fact that he continued to listen and learn helped his progress. On bowling a long hop on a wet surface at the Oval, which was duly dispatched for four by Surrey's Mike Willett, Page escorted him down the pitch, showed him the mark where the ball had landed and said, 'On a wet wicket always overpitch rather than pitch short,' advice he took very much to heart thereafter. Bowling short on any wicket was a hanging offence in his lexicon and should be avoided at all costs.

With pacemen Alan Brown and John Dye, leg-spinner David Baker and Page himself all among the wickets, Underwood was part of a penetrative attack that helped Kent to third place in the second XI championship. He had two more five-wicket hauls, but against Middlesex at Gore Court, Sittingbourne, he had to share the limelight with Knott. The *East Kent Gazette* commented, 'From Kent's view, two telling points emerged. The first concerned the performance of 16-year-old Erith schoolboy Alan Knott, who bowled 14 overs and finished with the very creditable figures of 2-26. Knott, who has plenty of time to develop, could well be Kent's foremost off-spinner in a few years' time.' Having kept wicket in a previous game against Northamptonshire at Aylesford, Knott had missed a stumping off Underwood before getting three off Baker against the Royal Engineers at Chatham, a performance that persuaded Les Ames that his future might lie with wicketkeeping rather than bowling. 'Underwood, a 17-year-old slow-medium left-hand bowler played regularly,' reported the *Kent CCC Annual*, 'and showed great promise by taking 42 wickets at an average of 19, his number of wickets being exceeded only by Baker who took 48.' Impressed with his efforts, the cricket sub-committee recommended an increase in his salary to £8 a week (and Knott's from £6 to £7 a week) as well as £40 of winter money.

He also had some success with the Colts, not least with his batting. Opening the innings with Alan Ealham against Kent Schools, they put on 100 for the first wicket, both scoring half-centuries, before Richard Burnett, watched by his grandfather Frank Woolley, one of the giants of the game, bowled his side to an innings victory.

In a year in which Underwood confirmed all the hopes Kent had placed in him, his most arresting image was that of Hampshire's 'Butch' White wearing his MCC touring jersey when playing against him. The sight of the distinctive red and yellow stripes enhanced his imagination and fuelled his ambition to follow in his footsteps.

Chapter 2

Teenage Prodigy

UNDERWOOD'S ARRIVAL at Kent coincided with a revival in the county's fortunes. For years they had languished in the lower reaches of the Championship table – between 1948 and 1963 they'd only twice finished in the top nine – their progress not helped by having four captains in five years. The appointment of Colin Cowdrey as captain in 1957 proved a pivotal point on the road to recovery. His first major initiative, securing the appointment of Les Ames, the former Kent and England wicketkeeper-batsman as secretary-manager, was one of the shrewdest moves he ever made. Aside from his business experience as a sports outfitter which helped to turn the club's small loss into a decent profit, Ames, with his steely personality, was the ideal foil to Cowdrey, particularly in matters of discipline. 'Colin was very good tactically on the field,' recalled David Clark, chairman of Kent's cricket committee, 'but he hated ticking off a player.' In contrast Ames was tough and would lay down the law in simple, uncompromising terms which left little room for misunderstanding.

Together with Cowdrey, Page and Lewis, Ames set out to identify the best young players in the county, and thanks to their sophisticated scouting system they unearthed a crop of exceptional talent: Underwood; Knott; batsmen Mike Denness, Brian Luckhurst and Alan Ealham; all-rounder Graham Johnson and fast bowler John Dye.

Although never claiming to know him well (he always refrained from calling him by his Christian name) Underwood was devoted to Cowdrey, one of his childhood idols, and always wanted to bowl in his net. 'One of the great features of his captaincy was the fact that everyone could identify with a great player, and they responded to that,' he later recollected. Living close to Underwood, Cowdrey used to chauffeur him to and from matches in his early years, spending hours talking to him about the game, his infectious enthusiasm readily apparent. Recognising a bowler of outstanding potential – and the kind he loved because of his ability to give nothing away over after over – Cowdrey encouraged him to the hilt, particularly on those days when he toiled for little reward. His willingness to bring him back against the lower order so that he could get a couple of cheap wickets did wonders for his morale. 'To me, he was always a giant of a man,' Underwood later told the cricket writer Stephen Chalke, 'and he carried me along on his shoulders every day. He was sympathetic, yet he made me realise that every ball had to count.'

Named 12th man for Kent's opening game against Somerset in 1963, Underwood was driven to Taunton by chairman Stuart Chiesman in his Rolls-Royce. He then travelled to the Oval to play in a second XI game against Surrey, but with the first team depleted by injuries, especially a serious car accident to seamer David Halfyard the previous year from which he hadn't recovered, he and batsman David Nicholls were sent to Hull to play against Yorkshire. At King's Cross station they were put in charge of the luggage, a traumatic experience for Underwood, since Peter Richardson, captaining in Cowdrey's absence, accused him of losing his case until he recalled taking it to his hotel room and failing to bring it down. In a rain-ruined game, Underwood, according to *Wisden*, 'made an impressive debut' with 4-40, his first victim being Ray Illingworth followed by Ken Taylor, Fred Trueman and Don Wilson, all of whom were England players in their time.

He kept up the good work in his first home game against Northamptonshire at Dartford, taking five wickets including the legendary Colin Milburn twice. According to Arthur Phebey, writing in the *Kent Herald*, 'In an attack that unfortunately has not been noted for its economy in recent years, he brings a refreshing accuracy to the proceedings. In this respect his figures at times have been remarkable.'

He graced his first appearance at Lord's with seven wickets, with England players Peter Parfitt and Fred Titmus numbered among his victims in both innings. 'Derek's left-arm medium pace, bowled with mature control, stamps him as one of the best prospects I have seen,' wrote the *Daily Mirror*'s Brian Chapman.

Bludgeoned by Sussex in the first round of the Gillette Cup – his figures of 0-87 off 11 overs were his worst ever in the one-day game – he recovered quickly to return his first five-wicket haul in an innings against Leicestershire. He continued to carry all before him, capturing ten wickets against Surrey at Blackheath and securing some notable scalps such as Basil Butcher, Seymour Nurse and Frank Worrell in Kent's match against the West Indies. Come the final game of the season – against Gloucestershire at Bristol – his tally of wickets stood at 94.

He captured four in the first innings in the home side's total of 105 and, after a blank second day, Kent scored quickly before Richardson declared. Given the new ball, Underwood responded by dismissing openers Ron Nicholls and Arthur Milton to reach his landmark, becoming the youngest-ever player to take 100 wickets in a debut season. He celebrated by hitting two sixes off Sam Cook in his undefeated 20, but Kent, needing 96 to win, lost by seven runs.

For all his accomplishments, not everyone hailed Underwood as the new Messiah. Former England all-rounder Trevor Bailey, dismissed by him on their first encounter for nought, told Les Ames he would prefer to wait another year to see if the batsmen would overcome his technique. 'I think this reluctance was mainly because no one had ever seen a left-hand bowler quite like Derek,' Ames later wrote. 'The older critics immediately made comparisons with the left-hand giants of the past such as Rhodes, Blythe, Woolley and Verity whereas in fact he was unlike any of these. He was much quicker through the air, not flighting the ball as the ones I have mentioned.'

Ames went on to say that the slow left-armers of his era were more inclined to buy their wickets by having a long-on and long-off and inviting the batsmen to have a go, in the hope that they would perish to a catch in the outfield. Underwood, in contrast, would opt for a one-saving field with two or three men up close for the catch.

Ignoring the sceptics like Bailey, Kent viewed matters rather differently. Describing an attack that lacked penetration, Arthur Phebey wrote, 'Underwood must rate as the finest young player we have had for a few years. He has a wonderful temperament, works hard at the game and apart from his bowling could well be batting at number five and six for the county in a couple of years,' a prediction that fell well wide of the mark.

Delighted by his progress, Kent increased his salary to £400 a year and gave him a mounted cricket ball in recognition of his achievement. Presenting the ball to him at Kent's 1964 annual general meeting, president Noel Baker remarked that Kent possessed two of the finest left-armers ever in Colin Blythe and Frank Woolley, and he hoped Underwood would emulate their feats. His behaviour on and off the field had been exemplary.

Underwood began 1964 where he left off, taking 7-97 against Yorkshire at Bradford as Kent won in the pouring rain with minutes to spare, their first win in the broad acres since 1930. His performance, which won him an ovation from the home crowd, ranked as one of his season's highlights. According to Fred Trueman, writing in *The People*, he disguised his slower ball very well adding: 'He never lost his length when we got after him at Bradford and there is certainly an amazing future for him.'

A mere three wickets in his next five games saw him dropped for Surrey's visit to Gravesend. Restored to the side after one game, he took 4-21 against Gloucestershire, followed by 6-39 against Warwickshire and, a month later, a career-best 9-28 against Sussex at Hastings, a ground that witnessed some of his most memorable achievements. On a dry, dusty pitch, the home side, set 301 to win, had been given a breezy start from opener Ken Suttle and despite losing Richard Langridge and Les Lenham to Underwood in his second over they reached 79/2 at lunch.

On resumption, Alan Oakman fell to Underwood, but the pivotal moment came when the enterprising Suttle padded up to fast bowler David Sayer and lost his off stump. With the effects of the heavy roller now wearing off and the ball beginning to turn alarmingly, Underwood ripped through the rest of the Sussex batting. According to *The Times*, 'Everything in this match was eclipsed by the remarkable bowling of Underwood, the young Kent left-hander, whose craft and accuracy laid Sussex's hopes in the dust.'

Yet for all his success, the sceptics were still not convinced. Playing against Kent at Canterbury shortly afterwards, Hampshire opener Roy Marshall was strolling round the ground after his dismissal by Underwood when he bumped into MCC president Gubby Allen. Allen asked him if he'd seen any young bowlers he'd recommend for his President's XI against the Australians, whereupon Marshall pointed to Underwood and said, 'There's a fine bowler for you.' Allen begged to differ. 'What's he got?' he countered. 'On a good wicket he's got nothing.' Marshall replied, 'He bowls a good length, he can turn the ball, and he varies his pace. What more do you need on a good wicket?'

Underwood continued to thrive in all conditions, not least in Dover Week with 6-43 against Northamptonshire, but while he caused Yorkshire some problems, he was overshadowed by a phenomenal performance from all-rounder Ray Illingworth. Having rescued Yorkshire with a superb 135, he sent Kent crashing to defeat with seven wickets in each innings.

On Thursday, 27 August there occurred a further milestone in Underwood's short career when he was awarded his county cap during Kent's game against the Australians in front of a capacity crowd at Canterbury. Having ensured that his parents were present, Cowdrey held up play and waved in the direction of the pavilion whereupon 12th man Mike Denness came out bearing the cap, which Cowdrey then presented to Underwood amid much acclaim. Somewhat miffed not to have received his cap the previous year, Underwood was delighted with the award, the second-youngest Kent player after Cowdrey to have achieved it, calling it the greatest thrill of his life, not least because it entitled him to another pay rise, this time to £575 per year.

Although subjected to a mauling from Australia all-rounder Tom Veivers, who hit 79 in 48 deliveries, Underwood had the last laugh by having him caught by wicketkeeper Knott off a skier to finish with 5-100. Earlier that summer, Knott had made his first-team debut against Cambridge University at Folkestone and in the next game Leicestershire's Paul Munden became the first victim of his celebrated partnership with Underwood. With former wicketkeeper Tony Catt moving to South Africa, Knott became Kent's permanent one in 1965, receiving his county cap that year, and after touring with MCC under-25s to Pakistan in 1966/67 he made his Test debut months later.

For the second successive season it was touch and go as to whether Underwood would reach 100 wickets. With Kent only 50 runs ahead of Somerset and half the side out at the end of the penultimate day of their final game, it looked as though he would miss out. However, captain Peter Richardson was equal to the situation with a ruse up his sleeve. Opening some bottles of champagne in the dressing room, he invited his opposite number Bill Alley to join them and told him that paceman Fred Rumsey, Kent's bogeyman in their second innings, shouldn't open the bowling the next day. If he did, Kent would simply play for a draw and not set Somerset a target.

Sure enough, Rumsey was nowhere to be seen the next morning when Alley began with spinners Brian Langford and Roy Kerslake. Kent accumulated steadily with Knott scoring 55 and by the time Rumsey returned to the attack, it was too late. Underwood made 33 and later celebrated his 100th wicket when bowling Mervyn Kitchen as Kent won by 52 runs. According to team-mate Bob Wilson, writing in the *East Kent Gazette*, 'Derek Underwood … proved his first season's performance of over 100 wickets was no fluke. And Underwood can still improve.

'While he has great control of length and direction, he is not yet able to bowl the cutter,' an ironic comment, since nothing annoyed Underwood more than being called a cutter rather than a spinner.

Having taken 100 wickets in 1964, along with Alan Dixon the first time two Kent bowlers had achieved this feat since 1950, 1965 proved less productive. Underwood wrote, 'Quite frankly I struggled that summer. For the previous two seasons I had been the new boy in the game. Batsmen were not quite sure what to expect or how to treat me. By my third year they had started to play me with a feeling of security, having learned my limitations.'

He came under pressure from Ames and Cowdrey to bowl over the wicket to help drift the ball towards the slips and the latter arranged a net session at his home, but the experiment proved unsuccessful. Underwood recalled that 'the result of that exercise in Colin's back garden was to convince me even more that I was better off bowling at my normal pace round the wicket with the umpire standing up'. To hit the off stump when bowling over the wicket, he had to pitch outside the leg stump to allow for the angle of delivery and if the ball turned, he would miss the off stump completely, often by a wide margin. On the other hand, bowling round enabled him to pitch wicket to wicket to get an lbw or pitch just outside the off stump and hit the wicket with the one that went with the arm.

After this slight stumble – although August brought him 11 wickets against Warwickshire at Edgbaston and nine against Essex at Leyton, giving him 89 for the season – 1966 saw Underwood scale the highest of peaks. In a damp summer of rain-affected pitches he preyed on batsmen throughout, helped by a new experimental rule restricting the first innings in 12 Championship games to 65 overs to encourage brighter cricket. Nothing better illustrated the greater risks batsmen took than when Kent hosted Gloucestershire at Folkestone, since five of Underwood's six victims were caught by Ealham, one of Kent's finest outfielders, at long-on. According to Les Ames, he'd never seen a fielder take five catches in the deep before; the fact that they were all in the same position made it even more unusual.

Beginning with a match tally of ten wickets against Middlesex at Lord's in his second game, he continued in prime form with 11 wickets against Somerset at Bath and 6-20 against Essex at Dartford. Three weeks after his 21st birthday, for which Cowdrey's wife Penny baked him a cake, he was picked for England to play against the West Indies, becoming the youngest Englishman to be capped since Brian Statham in 1951. Learning the news from his mother on returning to the family caravan at Whitstable from a Sunday afternoon watching cricket, he pronounced himself delighted. It was every English cricketer's ambition to play for his country and see the world.

His inclusion wasn't entirely welcomed. Deploring the lack of quality spinners, *The Times'* John Woodcock wrote,

'The departure of Titmus, after long and valuable service, was predictable; the arrival of Underwood, who bowls left arm over the wicket at slow-medium pace, may be attributed to the need for a left-arm bowler, rather than the belief that Underwood is worthy of his place.' In contrast, West Indies captain Gary Sobers, who'd read of his phenomenal record, viewed him as more of a threat. 'Obviously here was someone we would have to watch carefully,' he commented.

After suffering an innings defeat in the first Test at Old Trafford, England, under new captain Colin Cowdrey, had rallied sufficiently at Lord's to secure an honourable draw and the momentum continued at Trent Bridge. Although Underwood dropped opener Peter Lashley, England bowled their opponents out for 235 and established a lead of 90. Much of that was down to a century from Tom Graveney, 96 from Cowdrey and a last-wicket stand of 65 between D'Oliveira and Underwood. While D'Oliveira went for his shots Underwood displayed resilience against the West Indian quicks. Struck on the arm by a bouncer from Sobers, peeved about a run-out decision which went in the batsman's favour, he kept his cool and remained undefeated on 12 when D'Oliveira was bowled by Wes Hall for 76.

With West Indies in cautious mode as they knocked off the deficit, Underwood began with a slew of maidens, but although remaining economical in a long bowl after the weekend he went wicketless as a double century from Basil Butcher and 94 from Sobers put them out of sight. Losing wickets at regular intervals, England were on the cusp of defeat when Charlie Griffith unleashed a bouncer at Underwood, hitting him in the mouth. Describing the delivery in the commentary box, a horrified John Arlott exclaimed, 'No! No! No! It can't have happened.' After taking a few seconds to compose himself he said calmly, 'Griffith chucked a bouncer and hit Underwood in the teeth.' As West Indies fielders rushed to aid the stricken batsman and the crowd vented their fury the England team was no less forgiving. 'I have never known such a feeling of shock and anger to be common to so many players as when that happened,' recalled Graveney. 'For minutes the England dressing room seethed.'

Following a five-minute break in which Underwood received a glass of water – his partner John Snow told him not to spit it out on a length – he was able to resume his innings and hit both Griffith and off-spinner Lance Gibbs for four before Griffith bowled Snow to finish the game. West Indies had come from behind to record a satisfying victory by 139 runs, but their success was overshadowed by the injury to Underwood. Amid the widespread condemnation of Griffith, Brian Chapman described the incident as 'vicious and utterly uncalled for'; the *Daily Telegraph*'s E.W. Swanton wrote that the ball 'offended the convention whereby tail-enders are not threatened by bouncers' and *The Times*' John Woodcock stated ominously that the more he saw of Hall and Griffith's short-pitched bowling the less he liked it. According to D'Oliveira, Underwood was incapable of defending himself against the bouncer and that made it unfair. He wrote, 'I don't know what he thought of his first Test, but it couldn't have been too cheerful. He collected a split cheek, nought for 91 and a written apology from Charlie Griffith. In his place, I could have done without that lot.'

In response to the denunciation, Sobers wrote, 'I did not agree with bowling a bouncer at a number eleven, and told Charlie so, but I did not accept the view of some critics that it had been a deliberate act. Charlie never tried to hit anyone.

The bouncer is an accepted part of the game. The bowler uses it to unsettle batsmen, and there has never been any question of banning it, only of keeping its use within acceptable limits.

'Charlie felt he was entitled to try one on Underwood, because the Kent bowler had batted for 85 minutes in the first innings and helped Basil D'Oliveira add 65 valuable runs for the last wicket. Underwood was proving just as obstinate in the second innings. He was able to bat on and was 10 not out when England's final wicket fell.'

Whether Sobers asked Griffith to apologise to Underwood, as Griffith alleged, or whether he did it voluntarily, as Sobers claimed, he did. Playing for Kent against West Indies at Canterbury days later, Underwood was followed into the cloakroom by their manager Jeff Stollmeyer who, without saying a word, presented him with a letter of contrition from Griffith, who assured him that no harm was intended.

Returning to county cricket, Underwood continued to make headlines with 4-20 and 9-37 against Essex at Westcliff on the worst pitch he ever encountered. Opposing wicketkeeper Brian Taylor was hit on the glove and shoulder by the ball whereupon it dropped via his pads to hit the stumps. Had opener Gordon Barker been caught off him early in the second innings, Underwood reckoned that the match would have been over in one day. As it was, he'd taken all seven wickets to fall before the close and although Barker carried his bat for 36, the next morning, Essex were bowled out for 80, giving Kent victory by eight wickets.

He followed this with 7-50 against Worcestershire at Maidstone and when he bowled Lance Gibbs in MCC's President's XI v West Indians fixture he became the first man to reach 100 wickets for the season. 'Although he has run to 100 wickets before any other English bowler, Underwood had to send down 73 overs before dismissing a West Indian,' declared the yet-to-be-convinced Woodcock. 'There is a world of difference between the pitches he plays on in county matches and those of representative games, and between county opposition and West Indian opposition.'

Selected again for the fourth Test at Headingley, he gained his maiden Test wicket when Rohan Kanhai was caught by Graveney at silly mid-off, but that was his only success in a feckless England performance. Beaten by an innings, the critics clamoured for changes and Underwood was one of five players axed in the purge. On reflection, he thought his debut was premature, not least because Cowdrey had asked him to bowl over the wicket. 'But I wasn't totally happy about it; lbws were almost taken away from me. In my first Test I bowled all my overs over the wicket, and I look back at how appalling that was! After two Test matches, I had bowling figures of 1-170 and bagged a pair in my second Test. I went back to Kent and decided to go back round the wicket, and I had fantastic figures that year.'

While England were gathering at the Oval for the final Test, Underwood was destroying Lancashire at Blackpool with 6-9. Electing to bat first on a drying pitch, the home side were no match for Underwood's prodigious turn and lift as they collapsed to 62 all out. The young David Lloyd, batting at number eight, recalled the occasion. 'Underwood wasn't known as Deadly for nothing. From the angle of left arm round the wicket, the ball was flying over the batsman's shoulders, a most unnerving sight when you are padded up and waiting for your medicine. That was the kind of thing Underwood could do. Deliveries would explode off the surface and he would be absolutely unplayable.' When Lloyd asked the Lancashire captain Brian Statham for advice, he was told, 'I'd just have a swipe if I were you.'

In the final county game of the season at Harrogate, Yorkshire, the Championship favourites, doled out some punishment to Underwood in their first innings but after rain intervened, he took his revenge in their second innings. On a drying pitch and with his trousers tucked into his socks, he scythed his way through the formidable Yorkshire batting order, taking the first seven wickets for 17, leaving the game evenly poised at the close. Further overnight rain delayed the start and although Kent narrowly lost to the new champions their position of fourth in the table was their highest for 19 years. In addition, Underwood, the winner of the Cricket Writers' Club Young Cricketer of the Year Award for 1966, not only headed the national bowling averages with 157 wickets at 13.8, the first Kent cricketer to achieve this since Colin Blythe in 1914, his total of 144 wickets for Kent was also the highest for the county since Tich Freeman topped 200 in 1935. Greatness beckoned.

Chapter 3

National Hero

UNDERWOOD'S REWARD for such a productive season was selection for the MCC under-25 side to tour Pakistan under Mike Brearley which comprised future Test players such as Alan Knott, Pat Pocock and Keith Fletcher. The itinerary of eight games in five weeks was an arduous one, especially given the local climate, food and accommodation. When Underwood flopped down on his bed in the government rest house at Sahiwal it promptly broke. Rooming together with Knott in Chittagong he agreed to his request to have the fan on all night to combat the heat, but on waking the next morning his neck was so stiff that he couldn't turn his head. Compelled to miss some of the game against East Pakistan, he watched aghast as Alan Ormrod, an occasional bowler, took 4-32 on a rare turning wicket.

Up against a Pakistan side that included quality batsmen such as Asif Iqbal, Mushtaq Mohammad and Majid Khan, Underwood found it extremely difficult to adapt to the flat, grassless pitches. From the moment Pakistan's Shafqat Rana drove him for three silky boundaries in the first representative game at Lahore, he made little impression compared to fellow spinners Pocock and Robin Hobbs with their extra bounce and turn. It was during that game that Knott kept to him for a full session without one ball getting through to him and Underwood's low morale was further undermined when Brearley handed the ball to the part-time spinner Keith Fletcher against North Zone. 'He took 4-50,' Underwood wrote, 'and at one stage I felt like packing in the game completely as I stood at cover catching them off Fletcher.'

Explaining Underwood's lack of success, manager Les Ames commented, 'The trouble in Pakistan was that the wickets were so slow, and Derek was not able to turn the ball as he does not spin it all that much. There was almost no bounce, and the ball never got up more than about a foot from the ground, so when he did get an edge the ball did not carry to become a chance.'

'Underwood was a little disappointing,' wrote Brearley in *The Cricketer*. 'There was no bite in the wicket for his cutters and try as he would he often looked straightforward when genuine spinners beat the bat. But he was still invaluable for blocking up one end, was completely reliable, and bowled admirably without luck.'

Confronted with the first barren spell of his career, Underwood spent hours discussing his predicament with Knott, without finding an answer. At Brearley's suggestion, he tried bowling slower to deceive the batsman in the flight, but this didn't work because he lost his accuracy, yet despite his dejection, not helped by the poor accommodation and umpiring, he was indebted to his captain for all his understanding.

Back home, the pitches certainly aided him and his harvest of wickets for Kent (see later chapter) earned him a recall for the second Test against Pakistan at Trent Bridge, along with fellow spinner Fred Titmus. They replaced Illingworth and Hobbs, who'd played in the first four Tests of the summer. The match also saw the recall of Cowdrey and an international debut for Knott, thereby diminishing Kent's Championship prospects at a crucial stage of the season. With the England pace attack dominant on the first day, Underwood had little chance to prove himself, but his seven overs yielded the prize wicket of Pakistan captain Hanif Mohammad, who'd saved his side from defeat in the first Test with an undefeated 187. Having seen his second delivery driven for four, Underwood tossed the fifth one a little slower and Hanif mistimed it to cover.

In a game badly disrupted by the weather, Pakistan began their second innings on the final day on a drying pitch after water had seeped through the covers. Only Saeed Ahmed with an attractive 68 coped with the conditions until he became one of Underwood's five victims, the others including Mushtaq, lbw to his arm ball without scoring, and all-rounder Intikhab Alam caught by Knott, one of his six catches (and one stumping) that crowned a polished debut.

England, victors by ten wickets at Trent Bridge, won comfortably again at the Oval, despite a magnificent 146 from Asif, completing an unbeaten season for captain Brian Close. He seemed all set to lead MCC in the West Indies only to be held responsible for a serious breach of time-wasting in Yorkshire's Championship game against Warwickshire. At the insistence of MCC, he was replaced as captain by Cowdrey, but neither Cowdrey nor manager Les Ames favoured Underwood's selection, partly because of his record on the flat wickets in Pakistan, where Ames had been manager. 'Derek Underwood is also unfortunate to miss out and it was a near thing for him,' commented chairman of selectors Doug Insole. 'We had to weigh his merits overseas against others.'

Learning of his omission on his car radio on the way to play Essex at Dover, Underwood was devastated, calling it one of the great disappointments of his career. He later wrote, 'The choice of the third spinner rested between Pocock, who had not played in a Test match at that stage of his career, and myself who had the grand total of four Test appearances against my name. With Pocock in I knew I was out. And I was heartbroken.'

Buttressed by many a sympathetic comment from Kent supporters on his arrival at the ground, he was consoled by Cowdrey, who told him that his time would come and that finger-spinners rarely flourished in the Caribbean. 'The selectors believed that he wasn't the right type to succeed in the West Indies,' recalled Hobbs, who gained preference over him, 'but I had my doubts about that because I think Derek Underwood was successful on most pitches.' Having commiserated him on his omission, Hobbs in return was grateful for Underwood's best wishes. 'Derek was the first to congratulate me; he's never been any different. That takes a lot of doing.'

Knowing of Underwood's desire to broaden his experience of bowling in hot conditions, Cowdrey helped get him picked for a three-month tour of Africa and Asia by an International XI in the new year. Prior to that Underwood sought casual employment, the lot of the professional cricketer every winter. For his first two years at Kent, he worked for Ray Cox, the law stationers who'd employed his mother, then in 1965/66, he was employed by the Inner London Education Authority as cricket coach for Crystal Palace Recreation Centre and for the next two years before going on tour he was a PE instructor at Malory School in Lewisham. His arrival to teach games amazed pupils such as Brian Stater. He wrote, 'I recall him squelching around in the mud on the smelly football field we travelled to [it was next to a gas works in Catford] and talking to us as though we were adults which we certainly weren't. Oh, and he arrived each morning in a rusty old Peugeot, which he drove as though it was a Ferrari. No master at Malory was ever called "Sir" more enthusiastically than our Mr Underwood.'

The International XI under the leadership of Surrey captain Micky Stewart and comprising players such as Amiss, Denness and Fletcher, covered 32,000 miles and played 46 days of cricket in ten different countries. In two first-class games Underwood had figures of 9-53 against the Chief Minister's XI at Madras and 15-43 against the Ceylon President's XI at Colombo. Although Stewart reproached him for flighting a delivery on that drying Colombo pitch, saying 'Locky would never have bowled that ball,' Underwood warmed to his professional approach and the opportunity to visit many new places and stay privately with different hosts.

Back on home soil he was included in the 14 for the first Test against Australia at Old Trafford but omitted from the final XI as England, fearful of a dubious pitch, opted to play an additional batsman and only three front-line bowlers. According to Tom Cartwright, one of the bowlers discarded, 'It was an extraordinary decision not to play Derek. He was such a potent bowler at that time.' In the face of a crushing defeat, the selectors, resorting to a more balanced attack at Lord's, recalled Underwood and all-rounder Barry Knight. In a game decimated by bad weather he had little part to play until the final afternoon when Australia, following on, faced a torrid examination. Although the delayed start gave England little hope of victory, Underwood kept probing, bowling Ian Redpath and Doug Walters with his change of pace in an 18-over spell which yielded a mere eight runs.

England's improvement continued at Edgbaston. After Cowdrey had marked his 100th Test with a century, Underwood and Illingworth induced an Australian collapse in their first innings and they faced a challenging final day before they were once again saved by the weather.

An injury to Cowdrey gave former England captain Ted Dexter the chance to re-establish his Test credentials despite three years away from the first-class game. It was agreed that he would play in Sussex's next Championship game against Kent at Hastings, a formidable assignment, since he was confronted with a grassy pitch offering a fair amount of movement. With Sussex struggling at 27/4 and Underwood in the groove, Dexter played him off the front foot, employing a deftly relaxed grip on the bat handle to evade the crouching close-in fielders. Surviving until lunch, he loosened the shackles thereafter by dispatching the bowling to all parts, one six off Underwood ending up on the Town Hall roof.

Dexter later wrote, 'I had a good feeling as I walked out with my old brown, light bat to face Derek Underwood who was bowling on a pitch that should have suited him. Happily, I had a good record against the great Kent left-arm spinner. I had worked out that neither his quicker ball, nor his slower ball really turned. Thus, if I waited patiently before moving … I would see some good chances to score through the leg side for the quicker one, and off the back foot for the slower ball.

'Unfortunately for him, my eye was in, the form was there, and I started scoring runs right away. I was making minced meat of the Kent bowling and reached 100 quite comfortably.

In what must have been among my best-ever innings, I carried on until I'd passed the double century, when I was promptly caught for 203.

'It was a helpful pitch for Derek Underwood, as Hastings usually was,' said Sussex opening bowler John Snow. 'That was a challenge to Ted, and he played him so well it was as if he had never been away.' 'He gave Underwood hell,' commented all-rounder Tony Greig. 'I have never seen him punished so severely either before or since.'

Dexter's classic innings won him an immediate recall to Test match duty at Headingley. In a turgid game so reminiscent of Ashes contests of that era, Underwood was England's best bowler in Australia's first innings of 315. John Edrich and Roger Prideaux opened with a century stand but they let slip their advantage with some unenterprising batting before a capacity Saturday crowd. As Underwood walked to the wicket at 241/9, the groundsman was ready with his roller, but England's last man had other ideas. Taking advantage of the close-in field and a tiring attack, he hit lustily to leg with some crisp shots and dominated a stand of 61 with David Brown. When Brown was finally bowled by off-spinner Bob Cowper, Underwood returned to a rousing welcome from the Yorkshire faithful, undefeated on 45, his highest ever Test score. *The Guardian*'s John Arlott wrote: 'Suddenly after England's trials of the preceding three hours, batting appeared pathetically simple. On the easy pitch, Underwood generally found an appropriate pull, swing, sweep or safe edge for anything that came his way, and occasionally he varied his on-side bias with a smack through the covers.'

He kept his vice on Australia in the second innings but led by Redpath, who used his feet to him, and Ian Chappell, they batted long enough to gain them the draw they needed to retain the Ashes. Despite their disappointment England approached the final Test with purpose. After Cowdrey won the toss, their batsmen, led by centuries from Edrich and D'Oliveira, made hay on an easy-paced strip. Although Bill Lawry held them up with a seven-hour century, they gained a first-innings lead of 170 and chased quick runs on the fourth afternoon, leaving Australia 352 to win. They closed on 13/2 after Brown dismissed Lawry and Underwood had Redpath lbw to his arm ball, not offering a shot.

The next morning Underwood, now getting some assistance from the pitch, accounted for Ian Chappell, lbw to his quicker ball, and Walters, expertly caught by Knott off one that lifted. With Illingworth accounting for Paul Sheahan, Australia lunched precariously at 86/5 whereupon the heavens opened. A violent thunderstorm deluged the ground, leaving it under water within half an hour. As the Australians celebrated in their dressing room, thinking that once again the gods had spared them and the England players packed their kit disconsolately, Cowdrey had other ideas. Although the water was inch deep in places, he knew the Oval was an extremely quick-drying ground and was confident that, with a concerted effort, they would be playing again by 5pm. At his instigation an appeal was made for volunteers to help the groundstaff clear the surface water with buckets and brooms, and when hundreds responded he loitered in the middle to encourage them.

Thanks to their efforts, play duly commenced at 4.45pm. With only 75 minutes remaining Cowdrey went straight on to the offensive, by posting eight men round the bat, but the sodden pitch appeared so lifeless that neither Underwood nor Illingworth troubled John Inverarity and Barry Jarman, the

Australian batsmen. With time running out, Cowdrey threw the ball to D'Oliveira with a gambler's last throw of the dice. His hunch did the trick. In his third over he bowled Jarman playing no shot and with 35 minutes remaining, Cowdrey immediately recalled Underwood at the Pavilion End. Helped now by a drying pitch, he sent back Ashley Mallett and Graham McKenzie in his first over, both caught at short leg by David Brown off lifting deliveries.

Confronted with some dogged resistance from John Gleeson, Underwood went over the wicket, before switching back to round and with his first ball he bowled him, deceiving him with his change of angle. This left last man Alan Connolly to hold out for ten minutes with opener Inverarity, who was playing in only his second Test. Having defied the England bowlers for over four hours, Inverarity padded up to Underwood's arm ball with six minutes left and was palpably lbw. 'Sometimes you appeal when you hope it might be out, but I just knew with that one,' Underwood later recollected. 'It was a straight ball. And Charlie Elliott was a brave umpire. If it was out, he would give it. The finger went up. If you asked Inverarity to play that ball again, I'm sure he'd play it with ease. But he succumbed to the pressure.' Refuting the idea that the pitch was a vicious turner, Underwood continued, 'You'd think people would be getting caught at slip and gully, with the ball turning and bouncing, but it never did. It just got a little bit big at times, but it was going straight on with the arm.'

Amid scenes of jubilation, Underwood was mobbed by youngsters as he led his team-mates off the field before sheepishly acknowledging the jubilant crowd from the pavilion balcony. 'I was shattered at the end of it and felt no particular elation at the time,' he wrote in his 1975 autobiography *Beating the Bat*. 'My first desire was to get back to the dressing room, and I remember thinking to myself how peaceful it looked as I entered the deserted room.' Following the celebrations he met up with his family – his mother was very emotional – to enjoy a quiet dinner at a Bromley steak house, the calm before the storm, because on returning home the phone didn't stop ringing until the middle of the night.

Underwood's match-winning performance of 7-50, the last 4 for 6 runs and in 27 deliveries, captivated the nation and won him plaudits from all comers. According to Cowdrey, he made the batsmen play every ball, and his length was unerring, while former Australia captain Bobby Simpson admired his decision to quicken his pace to suit the slowness of the pitch. The esteemed Australian journalist Jack Fingleton thought he'd performed magnificently. 'Some say he bowls too fast. I do not agree. He changes his pace with a slower ball. His best attribute is that he is always attacking. He is a very good cricketer.'

Another accolade came his way when he was named one of *Wisden*'s Five Cricketers of the Year for 1969. 'Few young cricketers have made such a direct impact on their entry to first-class cricket as Derek Leslie Underwood,' wrote its editor Norman Preston. 'At the age of 23 this left-arm slow-medium-paced bowler of Kent may be said to be on the threshold of a great career in world cricket.'

On the back of his feats against Australia he was an automatic choice for MCC's proposed tour of South Africa, which was quickly cancelled owing to the refusal of its government to admit the Cape Coloured D'Oliveira. An alternative was arranged to Pakistan, a country racked by political instability and public disorder as opposition grew to the discredited military regime of Ayub Khan. Both at the time and in retrospect they should never have gone and in the case of Underwood he nearly didn't go because of his brother's life-threatening illness.

More academic than Underwood, Keith had spent three blissful years at the London School of Economics (LSE), gaining a 2.1 in Economics. Aside from playing hockey for the university, he captained its cricket team and London Universities, excelling as a fiery fast bowler. Through a friend of his father's, he then secured employment with Abu, a new Swedish fishing company, in Glasgow, and played cricket for Poloc, one of the leading cricket clubs in the West of Scotland.

A sufferer from asthma and hay fever from an early age, Keith was laid low with an internal ulcer that caused severe bleeding in January 1969. With his condition critical, Underwood visited him in the Victoria Infirmary, Glasgow, and felt minded to withdraw from the tour, but Keith insisted that he go and represent his country, an act of unselfishness that he always appreciated.

On arrival at Karachi after a brief stay in Ceylon (Sri Lanka), manager Ames and captain Cowdrey went straight into negotiations with the Board of Control for Cricket in Pakistan (BCCP) and agreed to their revised itinerary in Ayub's regional strongholds. Beginning with 6-22 in the opening game against the Pakistan Board of Control XI at Bahawalpur, Underwood was rested for the next game at Lyallpur whereupon he returned to Lahore with Hobbs. One day they were playing on their hotel's pitch and putt course when a demonstration started up close by. So concerned was the hotel manager that he hustled the surprised pair indoors, telling them this was an anti-American movement and 'the demonstrators might mistake you for Americans'.

They rejoined the team for the rain-ruined game at Sahiwal where the cold in the government rest home was so great that the players lit fires in their rooms, only to find the chimneys blocked and the smoke choking them. It was on returning from Sahiwal to Lahore on a bumpy road that Underwood's bag containing all his kit fell off the van. A lorry driver spotted it by the side of the road, picked it up, drove the 60 miles to Lahore and tracked down the MCC hotel, where he returned it.

The first Test at Lahore took place against a background of constant interruptions, some of which were violent as a noisy crowd clashed with police and armed guards patrolling with rifles at the ready. It was left to Pakistan opening batsman Aftab Gul, who was also a student leader, to quieten the crowd. After he was out to Underwood, he went over to one of the most raucous of the stands and managed to restore some calm. 'Here was a young man who, if he lifted his hand, could stop or start a riot,' commented Underwood.

Although England experienced some uneasy moments in their second innings, it was Pakistan who had more reason to be grateful for a draw.

From Lahore MCC flew to Dacca, a city in the grip of mob rule following the withdrawal of the army and the police. Following discussions with local student leaders, who now controlled the city, Ames resolved that the match should go ahead. It wasn't the most popular decision he'd ever made, but the students kept the crowd in check until the final day when they started hurling bricks at each other and shining mirrors in the eyes of the England close-in fielders so they couldn't see properly.

In reply to Pakistan's first innings of 246 England had collapsed to 128/7 before D'Oliveira, brought up on the uneven surfaces of the Cape, played one of his finest innings. Tenaciously supported by Snow, Underwood and Bob Cottam, he scored 114, giving England a narrow lead of 28. They then took three quick Pakistan wickets but skilfully though Underwood bowled for his 5-94 off 44 overs, a crucial missed catch and the slowness of the wicket combined to ensure another draw.

The intimidating atmosphere of Dacca, with the sound of perpetual gunfire and running the daily gauntlet of pickpockets as they made their way from the pavilion to the team coach outside the stadium, kept the tourists in a frazzled state. They returned to trouble-torn Karachi to find it even more turbulent than when they had left. Subjected to a nightly curfew and confined to their hotel, Underwood thought the situation 'quite ridiculous'. He was one of the younger players who approached vice-captain Graveney to register their concerns. In a heated discussion, Graveney relayed these fears to Ames and Cowdrey, but despite the worthless assurances from the BCCP about security, manager and captain felt duty-bound to go ahead with the final Test.

Their good intentions soon proved to be hollow when after two days of frequent interruptions a full-scale pitch invasion on the third day by politically motivated students put paid to Knott's first Test century and the tour. Following some difficulty extricating themselves from the ground, the England team returned to their hotel before they were ferried to the airport in a covert operation and rushed through formalities to board the London-bound flight. Several players applauded as their plane became airborne and as they crossed the Alps Colin

Milburn led the team in a rendition of 'The Green, Green Grass of Home'.

On arrival, Underwood was met by his father and Keith, who'd been convalescing at the family home. To see his brother well on the way to recovery meant more than anything to him. Humble and gentle with a willingness to help anyone, Keith was the perfect elder brother who Underwood leaned on for advice, especially on legal and business matters. With cricket remaining an all-consuming passion between them, he was always at his most relaxed in Keith's presence, his infectious laugh a sign that everything was all right with the world.

Chapter 4

'England's Umbrella'

ON SUNDAY, 25 May 1969, the day he had been officially appointed captain of England for the summer, Cowdrey snapped his Achilles tendon when playing for Kent against Glamorgan, incapacitating him for over three months. The selectors chose Ray Illingworth, Leicestershire's new captain, as a temporary replacement but exuding natural authority from the outset he remained permanently in charge, leading England 31 times between 1969 and 1973.

Raised in the hard school of Yorkshire professionalism, Illingworth was a tough, uncompromising all-rounder imbued with a win-at-all-costs ethic. A canny off-spinner with a model action, he possessed one of the shrewdest cricket brains imaginable and, backed up by a brilliant fielding outfit at Yorkshire, he invariably proved a match-winner on damp or turning pitches. With his invaluable batting in the middle order, especially in a crisis, he performed the double of 1,000 runs and 100 wickets for the first time in 1957 and made his England debut against New Zealand the following year. Less effective on overseas wickets because of his lack of flight compared to off-spinners Fred Titmus and David Allen, Illingworth made little impression in the West Indies in 1959/60 and Australia in 1962/63 and for the next several years he was rarely picked by England. He continued, however, to be the lynchpin of the great Yorkshire side of the 1960s, not only with his all-round performances but as an astute mentor to captain Brian Close. An honest, forthright person who bristled at the insensitive treatment accorded to professional cricketers by the game's authorities, he fell out with Yorkshire chairman Brian Sellers and his refusal to grant him a three-year contract in 1968 prompted his departure from the club.

Yorkshire's loss was Leicestershire's gain. Teaming up with their enterprising secretary-manager Mike Turner, Illingworth willingly took on the captaincy and within weeks had injected a new, more positive spirit in the team that impressed the England selectors enough to award him the captaincy once Cowdrey became indisposed. Galvanised by his promotion, leadership brought the best out of him as a player. Having constantly failed with the bat at Test level, he now hit a century in his second game in charge and thereafter proved the most resolute of performers in the late-middle order.

He quickly asserted his authority over his players, especially the more contentious ones such as Boycott and Snow, dropping the latter after three Tests for failing to bowl as commanded. He also lay down the law to them on arrival in Australia in 1970, reminding Boycott that he wasn't the only batsman in need of practice and censuring Snow for his lack of effort in a state game. Having made his point, he had their full cooperation thereafter and both proved pivotal to England regaining the Ashes.

Like so many of his England team-mates, Underwood admired Illingworth's tactical nous, his unflappability under pressure and the ability to get the best out of his team. He wrote, 'Illingworth looked after his players. He was always willing to tackle the authorities on their behalf and insisted on the best for his team.' When Underwood was jeered by the Hill at Sydney for dropping a catch, Illingworth moved him to another position away from his detractors. He also sympathised with his reluctance, and that of other players, to attend social functions during the middle of a Test and he tried to restrict them to a minimum.

As a hard-headed professional who loathed giving the batsmen anything, Underwood enjoyed bowling in tandem with Illingworth, knowing there would be no cheap runs at the other end, and it is notable that in many of his finest performances for England – the Oval 1968, Lord's 1969 and Headingley 1972 – Illingworth played the support role to perfection. That said, Underwood only played in 20 of the 31 games Illingworth was in charge despite taking five wickets or more in an innings on seven occasions. While admiring Underwood's accuracy, stamina and his refusal ever to give up, Illingworth thought that on firmer pitches he lacked the turn of an index finger-spinner because he bowled too fast. Underwood, in turn, deprecated Illingworth's reluctance to bowl himself on a flat pitch, leaving him to shoulder the burden, and his tendency to set too attacking a field for him, compared to Cowdrey, whose field placings he thought were masterly.

On a personal note, Underwood sympathised with Cowdrey's emollient character and rallied to his side when he fell out with Illingworth in Australia, especially the captain's trenchant approach towards manager David Clark over player remuneration or his on-the-field clashes with Australian umpire Lou Rowan, whom Underwood called 'extremely charming'.

Underwood played in Illingworth's first game in charge, a convincing ten-wicket win against Gary Sobers's West Indies, in which he bowled tidily – two wickets for 46 off 31 overs – only then to be dropped for the Lord's Test, an omission which John Woodcock described as a howler.

Following the draw at Lord's, he was restored for the final Test at Headingley. Played for the most part in overcast conditions, batsmen on both sides struggled until the sun shone on the fourth day when West Indies, set 303 to win, seemed destined for victory, before Underwood intervened. Having already dismissed Charlie Davis and Steve Camacho, he made the crucial breakthrough at 219/3 when he had top scorer Basil Butcher caught by Knott for 91. By the time he dismissed his Kent team-mate John Shepherd, also caught by Knott, four wickets had fallen for nine runs and England went on to win a close game by 30 runs, giving them the series 2-0.

The New Zealand side that followed in the wake of West Indies appeared confident of posing a stiffer challenge to England than their two predecessors in 1958 and 1965 but, exposed to some testing conditions, they proved no match for Underwood. Confronted with a curious mottled pitch at Lord's on the morning of the first Test, Illingworth sought Boycott's advice on what he should do if he won the toss. Boycott told him that as a batsman he hoped he would insert the opposition but if he were making the decision he would bat first because Underwood would bowl them out in the second innings. Illingworth duly followed his advice and although England only made 190, they gained a narrow first-innings lead as he and Underwood imposed a stranglehold on the New Zealand batsmen. In their second innings Underwood was even more devastating, his 7-32 central to England's 230-run victory. After the game opposing captain Graham Dowling denounced the Lord's pitch but while it fell below Test standard it wasn't venomous, and Underwood thought that the New Zealanders had contributed to their demise by being unduly defensive.

It was a measure of his mastery that their batsmen were no better combating his wiles in the final Test at the Oval when, admittedly, the weather did them no favours. On winning the toss they made a solid enough start through opener Glenn Turner, who'd carried his bat at Lord's, and Bev Congdon, only then for a heavy shower to liven up the pitch. Once Underwood removed both batsmen, caught at slip by Phil Sharpe, he and Illingworth ran through the remainder, dismissing them for 150.

After England gained a lead of 96 on first innings, he had to work harder for his wickets in the second innings until the lower order succumbed to a plethora of rash strokes. One of his victims was all-rounder Bruce Taylor, who attempted to sweep him and played over the top of the ball. He did not appear to be stretched uncomfortably, but Knott went through his stumping drill, and when he looked at the crease Taylor's foot had dragged in front of the line and he was out.

Underwood's match figures of 12-101, the best return by an England bowler against New Zealand, was primarily responsible for his country's eight-wicket victory. Reviewing England's 2-0 series win and Underwood's 24 wickets at 9.16, *The Guardian*'s John Arlott wrote: 'Increasingly he seems able to make any pitch less than perfect a killing ground.'

With no official MCC tour that winter, Underwood toured the West Indies with both the International Cavaliers and the

Duke of Norfolk's XI, captained by Colin Cowdrey. Fellow team-mate Mike Griffith, who was captain of Sussex, recalls him as a very friendly, straightforward person, not particularly sociable, who lived for his cricket. Yet underneath that placid exterior there lurked a man with strongly held views.

While Underwood performed respectably in the first-class games against the islands, there were no dramatic figures on those flat pitches, a pointer to his struggle there on the 1973/74 MCC tour.

Back home, Underwood prepared for an exacting summer against South Africa. That tour, however, was cancelled owing to political pressure and an alternative series arranged against a Rest of the World XI led by Gary Sobers. Bowling to some of the world's leading batsmen on firm pitches proved a taxing proposition and after seven wickets in the first three games, almost all top-order batsmen, he was dropped in favour of Yorkshire's Don Wilson. Wilson, an orthodox left-arm spinner who partnered Illingworth for many years, was taken to Australia because of doubts about Underwood's ability to succeed on those flat wickets, but he failed to make any impact other than to come up with the nickname 'Deadly' following press speculation that Underwood would be deadly on a certain wicket.

He remained a certainty for the winter tour to Australia and New Zealand under Illingworth, whose assertive leadership over the past year won him the nod over arch-rival Cowdrey. Before departure, Underwood travelled to Glasgow with his family to act as best man to his brother Keith at his wedding to Anne McGuire, the accounts clerk in his company. At his jovial stag do at Poloc Cricket Club, Leslie Underwood out-drank the Scots with whisky and when Derek's then girlfriend arrived at the end of the evening to collect him the inebriated gathering thought she was a stripper.

Assembling a strong party, Illingworth expressed great confidence that he had the means to regain the Ashes, but their tentative start didn't suggest this. Informed that MCC had picked three spinners for the trip, Tony Lock, now captaining Western Australia, said, 'What spinners? Underwood, Wilson and Illingworth can't turn the ball in English conditions, so what hope have they got out here? Taking wickets in Australia is hard work. I can't see these three having any success.'

Without a win in four first-class games and defeated by Victoria, England began the series very much as underdogs, a sentiment confirmed by Australia's confident start. Winning the toss at Brisbane, opener Keith Stackpole enjoyed a great piece of luck on 18. Attempting a quick single, he failed to beat Boycott's direct throw to the bowler's end and was run out by some distance, but umpire Rowan gave him not out, much to the consternation of Boycott and Underwood, who'd dashed to the stumps to take the return.

Exploiting his luck to the full, Stackpole launched an assault on his opponents. As Underwood began his spell with several maidens, Cowdrey at first slip began a series of signals which followed each ball, telling him to slow down and place more faith in flight. He did so only for Boycott to drop Stackpole on 51 and, once again trading on his good fortune, the latter targeted Underwood, thrashing him for four boundaries in five deliveries. His 207 helped his side to 372/3 but Underwood returned fire, sending back Walters, Sheahan and Redpath in seven balls, dismissals that brought a smile to his face for the first time on tour, according to former Australia leg-spinner Bill

O'Reilly. Australia lost their last seven wickets for 15 runs. Their collapse tilted the game England's way. They went on to make 464, a lead of 31, and get the better of a draw.

Left out of the side in favour of an additional fast bowler for the second Test at Perth, Underwood would have been a useful addition in another high-scoring draw. The attritional nature of the cricket frustrated MCC manager David Clark and his comment that he would rather see England lose the series 3-1 than have all the Tests drawn exposed a rift within the team. Clark, an experienced administrator and an amateur of the old school, was appointed manager on the assumption that his protégé Cowdrey would be captain. The fact that Cowdrey missed out to Illingworth left Clark with a captain whose hard-nosed professionalism stood in direct contrast to the amateur tradition of attacking cricket and diplomatic niceties. Unhappy with Clark's comments, Illingworth clashed with him again over the revised itinerary following the abandonment of the third Test at the Melbourne Cricket Ground (MCG) owing to incessant rain. Without consulting his captain, Clark acceded to the Australian Cricket Board's (ACB) request to restructure the tour to accommodate an additional Test. His gesture found little favour with Illingworth and the players, who were already dissatisfied with their parsimonious meal allowances, the formal dress code and the number of receptions they were expected to attend.

Apart from objecting to the lack of additional remuneration, they disliked the revised schedule which required them to play four Tests in six weeks, during the hottest time of the year, which they thought would jeopardise their chances of winning the series. A team meeting was called in the captain's room and

Illingworth's line was endorsed by everyone (Cowdrey refused to attend) except Underwood, who maintained that playing for England was enough of an honour.

For the fourth Test at the Sydney Cricket Ground (SCG), Underwood, back in the side, proved his worth on what became one of his favourite Test venues. Assailed initially by Walters and Redpath that led to his removal from the attack, he marked his return by catching Greg Chappell, a centurion in his maiden Test in Perth, off his own bowling.

When the match resumed after the rest day, Underwood, extracting some turn from a slow, wearing pitch, accounted for Stackpole, Rodney Marsh and Ashley Mallett in seven overs as Australia lost their last six wickets for 49. Building on a lead of 96, a flawless 142 not out from Boycott placed England in an unassailable position before magnificent bowling by Snow on an uneven surface sent their opponents crashing to a 299-run defeat.

After two high-scoring draws on docile surfaces at Melbourne and Adelaide the two teams returned to the SCG for the final Test, England without Boycott, who'd broken his arm in an inconsequential one-day game. Inserted by Australia's new captain Ian Chappell, Illingworth's men could only manage 184 but struck back to have Australia 66/4. The home side rallied with a fifth-wicket stand of 81 between Redpath and Walters before Underwood, in what E.W. Swanton called his most valuable contribution to the tour, accounted for them both.

As Greg Chappell and Terry Jenner edged Australia into the lead, the game descended into acrimony when Snow felled the latter with a bouncer. While the crowd voiced its disgust captain Illingworth became engaged in a heated altercation with umpire Rowan in his reaction to the latter's warning of Snow for intimidatory bowling. In an increasingly raucous atmosphere, which saw some bottles thrown on to the field and Snow manhandled by a drunk in the crowd, Illingworth unilaterally led his team off the field, claiming their safety was under threat. It needed a warning from the umpires that England were in danger of forfeiting the match to bring about their return.

In a calmer atmosphere, England made 302 in their second innings, leaving Australia 223 to win. They soon lost the services of Snow, who dislocated his finger on the boundary pickets trying to catch Stackpole, but Illingworth kept his cool and chipped away at the Australian batting. On 123/5 overnight, they soon lost Marsh the next morning clean bowled by Underwood as he aimed for Bondi Beach and Greg Chappell neatly stumped by Knott as he advanced down the wicket to Illingworth. D'Oliveira then accounted for Kerry O'Keeffe and Dennis Lillee and when Underwood had Jenner caught close in by Fletcher England had triumphed by 62 runs to regain the Ashes after 12 years.

'Underwood did little to develop the guile necessary on true batsmen's pitches and he rarely threatened to take wickets, except when conditions were reasonably favourable to his bowling in Sydney,' wrote the acerbic E.M. Wellings in *Wisden*, but this underestimates his significance. A stickler for accuracy, he toiled away on some unblemished surfaces, giving England's strike bowlers much-needed respite and his contribution to his side's two victories was crucial. According to Illingworth, Underwood bowled splendidly, 'especially when we were trying to keep things tight. He bowled with marvellous control, got us the odd wicket and then we were able to throw Snowy back again.' From an Australian perspective, Walters, dismissed 12 times by Underwood in Tests, wrote, 'Not everyone rates Underwood so highly as a bowler, but I certainly do: I'd list him in the top five bowlers in the world today because, technically, he is almost perfect. It was difficult to look at him when the MCC arrived in Australia and say that bowling at that pace, he would take a lot of wickets on the tour. However, most people agreed that, by the time the series between England and Australia was over, he had played one of the most valuable parts in England's challenge for the Ashes.'

After slogging it out in Australia, Underwood had it easier in New Zealand. Presented with an under-prepared pitch in the first Test at Christchurch, he bowled England to a seven-wicket victory with figures of 6-12 and 6-85. On dismissing Michael Shrimpton in the second innings, he claimed his 1,000th first-class wicket, the third-youngest to achieve this landmark after George Lohmann and Wilfred Rhodes. The match was notable for the omission of Knott, much against his will, to give his loyal deputy Bob Taylor a game. Making his Test debut on such a fiendish pitch with the ball flying in all directions proved challenging, but he won Underwood's admiration by keeping immaculately.

Knott's temporary demotion spurred him on to even greater things because his 101 and 96 ensured his side a draw in the second Test at Auckland. Bowling on a flat pitch this time and feeling shattered at the end of a long tour, Underwood reckoned his 5-108 off 38 overs ranked as superior to his performance at Christchurch. Most of his wickets were gained through variation in flight and when he had Shrimpton lbw, he took his 100th Test wicket.

Illingworth's men returned to a royal reception, but the aura soon faded, since in a cool, damp summer the twin series against

Pakistan and India failed to capture public interest. Entering the first Test at Edgbaston without Snow, who was injured, the attack lacked penetration on a prime wicket and led by a sublime 274 from Zaheer Abbas, Pakistan made 608/7. Forcing England to follow on, they were well on their way to victory only to be denied by the weather.

Unimpressed with their performance, the critics rounded on Underwood who, after taking 7-28 against Yorkshire in Kent's opening Championship fixture, had endured three lean games in succession. Admitting that he was concerned about him, Ken Barrington, writing in the *Daily Mail,* thought he'd been overbowled and was showing the effects of five years of almost continuous cricket. According to the *Daily Mirror*'s Peter Laker, he bowled too fast and flat at Edgbaston to worry Pakistan's quick-footed batsmen and Swanton wrote that he must have distressed the purists since he bowled to a semi-circular field of eight men more or less equidistant, theoretically saving one, with only one slip.

'Underwood as on the first day, persisted tirelessly, first round then over the wicket, at a speed which precluded any hope of turn. Strange though it may seem to say so of a man with more than 100 Test wickets, Underwood in this sort of situation, at home as well as abroad, gives an impression of immaturity. It is worth noting that he will be only 26 on Tuesday: the same age, in fact, as Verity when he first played for England.'

When Underwood was duly omitted for the next Test, Swanton thought that no one would view his eclipse as other than temporary and that he would in time double his present tally of 107 Test wickets, 'Yet he does need more flexibility and "air" on plumb pitches.' Woodcock, in contrast, felt he was made the scapegoat for England's failure to bowl out Pakistan at Edgbaston and while accepting that on good wickets he had his limitations, England's opponents were delighted whenever he failed to make the side.

Devastated about his omission, especially since he thought he'd bowled well, going at little more than two runs an over, the most economical of the six bowlers used, Underwood suspected that the media criticism had influenced the selectors. He later wrote: 'The only thing that grated was the way the press pigeon-holed me as a "wet-wicket bowler", saying that I was like an umbrella to be carried around, just in case it rained. The implication was that I was no good on dry pitches, which I do not think was fair.'

He was replaced by fellow left-arm spinner Norman Gifford, who'd last played for England in 1964. 'The substitution of Gifford for Underwood will surprise many,' declared John Arlott in *The Guardian*. 'They both tend to bowl flat and if Gifford is a little slower and perhaps spins the ball – in terms of pure finger spin – more than Underwood neither of them has much flight. As batsmen and fielders, they are similar and in fact the change would have done little to alter the tactical balance of the team.'

'At that time there was little to choose between Derek and Norman, but Norman spun it more,' recalled Illingworth. 'Derek wasn't spinning it off the straight and we were carrying him around for wet wickets that never materialised.'

Gifford vindicated his selection with 14 wickets in the next three Tests, but to play three spinners – himself, Illingworth and Hobbs – on a slow turner at Headingley against Pakistan without one of them being Underwood seemed bizarre.

Gifford's broken finger, sustained in the second Test against India, enabled the in-form Underwood to regain his place for the final game at the Oval. On a slow turning pitch, England's first innings of 355 looked useful when they bowled India out for 284, with Illingworth taking 5-70, although several critics thought he'd mishandled Underwood by not bowling him from the end that was helping the spinners.

Having established a lead of 71, England threw away their advantage by batting recklessly against Bhagwat Chandrasekhar's leg spin and were shot out for 101, leaving India 173 to win. Snow accounted for Gavaskar without scoring and Underwood dismissed Ashok Mankad, superbly caught at slip by Richard Hutton, before captain Ajit Wadekar and Dilip Sardesai saw them safely through to stumps.

On the final morning when India needed another 97 for victory – they had never won in England – Illingworth encouraged Underwood to bowl a bit slower. He responded by dismissing Sardesai – brilliantly pouched by Knott off one that lifted – and catching Eknath Solkar off his own bowling, but after lunch he bowled too flat and defensively when flight was needed. Although restricted by some accurate bowling, especially from Illingworth, the sixth-wicket pair of Viswanath and Farokh Engineer remained in control, and the latter saw India home by four wickets, much to the acclaim of their fellow countrymen. As Illingworth mulled over his first defeat as captain of England, he reckoned they would have won the game had Gifford been fit.

Given the predilection of his captain, it was no surprise that Gifford was preferred to Underwood for the first three Tests against Australia the following summer, but after only one wicket he made way for Underwood at Headingley. According to Denis Compton in the *Sunday Express*, 'Derek Underwood to my mind is a much better prospect. He can be quite devastating if he gets a dusty or wet wicket to bowl on. And on a good wicket, he is so much quicker through the air and is more accurate than Gifford.'

After England's win at Old Trafford and Australia's at Lord's thanks to a remarkable 16 wickets on debut by opening bowler Bob Massie, the third Test at Trent Bridge was drawn, leaving the series finely balanced at Headingley. It was a game mired in controversy because of the state of the pitch. Australian's former captain Richie Benaud recalled commentating on the Yorkshire–Warwickshire match there three weeks earlier on a superb strip, but exceptionally heavy rain the weekend before the Test had flooded the playing area and water had infiltrated the covers. As a result of this continued covering, the groundsman discovered too late that a plant disease called fusarium had infected the pitch, killing off much of the grass, making it look more like Kanpur than Headingley. (Later the Test and County Cricket Board's pitches committee exonerated the groundsman George Cawthray of any incompetence or sharp practice.) Australia captain Ian Chappell recalled that the day before the Test his vice-captain Keith Stackpole suggested that he look at the pitch. 'I reminded him I only looked on the first morning of the match. "Well," said Stacky, "you'd better look at this one." When we reached the middle Stacky threw a ball hard into the surface of the pitch and it bounced no higher than his toe. When he repeated the exercise on the lush green strip next to the one for the match, the ball bounced to chest height.' Inspecting the pitch later that day, Illingworth and Jack Fingleton both thought it would be slow and true, a view similar to the *Yorkshire Post*'s J.M. Kilburn. On the opening day of the Test, he wrote that 'expectations are that in fine weather the pitch will offer runs in plenty. Yesterday's sun and breeze dried the turf which was flooded at the weekend and further drying should give it comfortable pace and durability.'

Chappell, on winning the toss, batted first and despite losing Ross Edwards for a duck, he and Stackpole took the score to 79/1 at lunch. In the first over afterwards Underwood bowled a delivery to Stackpole which reared dangerously from a good length to beat the outside edge and Knott took it high above his head to the right. The next ball Stackpole, playing forward, got a fine edge and Knott caught it some six inches from the turf, a catch that astounded Australia off-spinner, Mallett. He wrote, 'I have never seen keeping like it; the presence of Knott to stay low given the previous ball and kicking like a runaway colt simply blew me away.'

Stackpole's dismissal for 52 heralded a dramatic collapse whereby six wickets fell for 18 runs. While Illingworth accounted for Ian Chappell and Walters, Underwood trapped Greg Chappell lbw with his arm ball, tempted Rodney Marsh into a wild slog and had Paul Sheahan acrobatically caught by Illingworth at silly point. In a lengthy spell of 31 overs from the Football Stand End, he conceded a mere 37 runs. Calling it a slow turning pitch, Kilburn praised the craft of Underwood and Illingworth, who 'exposed all the Australian batting anxiety and infirmity … they played on fears and accumulated success from success.'

'Underwood found Australian pitches unyielding to bowl on,' wrote Fingleton in *The Times*. 'Yesterday he was in his element. He has an ideal pace for a pitch that gives him any assistance because he does not give a batsman any chance to change his mind. For much of his spell he had five men up close. His bowling was full of length, direction and guile. I value him highly.' Reviewing Australia's prospects, he concluded, 'We have nobody anywhere near the ability of Underwood and Illingworth as spinners, unless I underrate Mallett.'

All out for 146, Australia reduced England to 128/7 but an eighth-wicket partnership of 104 between Illingworth and Snow put the home side back in control. In front of a capacity Saturday crowd, Underwood entered the attack in the 11th over with the score at 31/2 and bowled 21 consecutive overs to five men around the bat. With his fourth ball he induced Greg Chappell into a reckless pull that spooned up to mid-on, before getting Stackpole lbw with one that straightened. After lunch he sent back Walters with a brute of a ball that turned sharply and lifted, had Marsh caught down the leg side by Knott and Inverarity taken at silly point by Illingworth, before bowling Lillee all ends up. By the time he took his sweater his 6-45 had sealed Australia's fate.

Following England's nine-wicket victory and their retention of the Ashes, the recriminations began in earnest. While the Australian players seethed in private, dumbfounded that the fusarium seemed to occur only on a stretch of turf 22 yards long by about eight feet wide, their press corps recalled the dust bowls at Old Trafford in 1956 where Laker had eviscerated them and at Headingley in 1961. Sid Barnes, one of Bradman's 1948 Invincibles, wrote in the *Sydney Sun* that the 1956 Australians under Ian Johnson had 'copped a dose of English sportsmanship'.

'Let's face it, they robbed us then when they were scared stiff of Lindy [Lindwall] and Nugget [Miller] and make no mistake they're doing the same thing now, because Lillee and

Massie turned all their grey-haired champions white and around the hairline as well as the gills.'

In an open letter to MCC secretary Billy Griffith, John Dunn, sports editor of the *Melbourne Herald*, wrote in exaggerated tones, 'We're not suspicious people but there is one aspect of this whole business which is puzzling. It concerns Derek Underwood.

'For most of your summer he has been in the cricketing wilderness, performing only moderately in the county games and not even getting close to the first 13 in the other Tests.

'Then, after Australia wins at Lord's and morally wins at Trent Bridge, out of the trees comes Underwood, a surprise selection to say the least. And what is more surprising, finds a pitch which his own father would have been embarrassed to prepare. Please assure me, Mr Griffith, so that I can pass it on to the cricketing public here, that it was just an extraordinary coincidence. It will stop a lot of talk.'

Australian grievances won some sympathy from their English counterparts. Fred Trueman labelled the pitch a disgrace in *The People* and Bill Bowes, the former Yorkshire fast bowler, said he'd never seen one like it at Headingley in 40 years; Arlott described it as far below the standard expected of a Test match, Swanton called it an embarrassment and Fingleton, always a balanced critic, wrote, 'Some of our batsmen abdicated yesterday with not much dignity but this was a tough pitch for them against Underwood and Illingworth.' Even Kilburn, while not surprised by the lack of pace in the pitch since this had been a feature at Headingley for years, acknowledged that it had failed to serve its purpose, not because of its early dampness but because the drying seemed to roughen the surface to leave the spin bowlers dominant. That said, he thought the Australians were out of their depth in such conditions and had contributed to their demise with some unworthy shots.

As far as Illingworth was concerned, any suggestion of chicanery by the ground authorities to suit England was 'absolute nonsense'. 'It is true that it was the sort of pitch to which English batsmen are very much more accustomed than the Australians are, and it posed problems of technique which were certainly searching ones for the Aussies. And it was the sort of pitch on which Underwood has, for many years, been the best bowler in the world.'

'With merciless persistence, impeccable length and questioning spin, he [Underwood] kept at them,' wrote Woodcock. 'It was altogether too much for batsmen already dispirited by that partnership of Illingworth and Snow.' According to the *Sunday Telegraph*'s Michael Melford, 'It is hard to believe that anyone could bowl better on a slow turning pitch than he did, turning the ball varying amounts at mostly his brisk medium pace,' while in Snow's estimation, Australia should have won the game because they had the best of the conditions when batting first, 'but try telling that to an Australian and he looks at you in disbelief. I was in Australia the following winter… and everywhere I went the subject of Headingley came up. The Australians just would not accept that they were beaten fairly and squarely, although I suspect Keith Stackpole recognised the truth. At the end of the match, he was very bitter about the Australian batting performance in both innings.'

Consumed by a sense of injustice, Australia approached the Oval Test with a burning ambition to win. On an excellent strip they took the early honours by bowling England out for 284 and reaching 274/3 by the end of the second day. As Ian Chappell drove Underwood to distraction by constantly sweeping him, a West Indian supporter of Australia called out from the crowd, 'Bad-wicket bowler. Don't let him get you out!' With both Chappells scoring centuries, the first time two brothers had achieved this in the same innings of a Test, Australia gained a first-innings lead of 115, although four late wickets for Underwood kept England in the hunt.

After 90 from opener Barry Wood and a second half-century in the game from Knott, Australia required 242 to win. They received a flying start from Stackpole, who found batting much easier once he'd scattered Underwood's close-in field. With Snow suffering from flu and Illingworth indisposed on the last day because of a twisted ankle, the visitors resumed in a commanding position, only to experience a mid-innings wobble. While Greig sent back Stackpole and Edwards, Underwood had Ian Chappell caught off a sweep and Greg Chappell lbw after one of his lifters had struck him in the throat, but that was his final success. After a period of consolidation, Sheahan and Marsh hit him to all parts as his line began to waver and their unbroken partnership of 71 gave Australia a well-merited five-wicket victory.

With a gruelling eight-Test tour of India and Pakistan that winter ruling out Illingworth, Boycott, Edrich and Snow, it was a relatively inexperienced side that assembled under Tony Lewis. Lewis had yet to play for England, but he'd led Glamorgan to the County Championship in 1969 and his affable personality helped forge a real camaraderie on tour, the most enjoyable Underwood went on. 'Tony was a charmer,' he wrote. 'Lively, full of fun, marvellous off the field and determined on it. He had not got quite the tactical appreciation of the other England captains with whom I have served but was most approachable in every way.' Team spirit also was accentuated by the absence of facilities up country, forcing the players to make their own entertainment and perhaps it is no coincidence that many of them, such as Amiss, Fletcher, Greig and Pocock, were among Underwood's closest cricketing friends.

Touring India with its millions of passionate cricket fans proved a real eye-opener. Lewis recalled Underwood, Wood and him getting a lift back to their hotel from practice with Farokh Engineer and how Engineer's car was surrounded by scores of locals, some of whom clambered on to the roof. Confronted with a raucous crowd of 35,000 for their opening game at Hyderabad, Underwood once stopped halfway through his run-up when startled by a firework.

On another occasion, playing for MCC against East Zone at Jamshedpur, he and Arnold were bombarded with stones by irate spectators after a six by local hero Rusi Jeejeebhoy was signalled a four by Arnold, who was irked that the batsman hadn't walked for a catch close to the wicket. Standing warily 20 yards in from the third man boundary as the missiles continued to rain down, Underwood's pleas to stop the carnage fell on deaf ears until steel-helmeted police restored order. Most bizarre of all was his experience at the end of the second Test at Calcutta. Lying in the bath in his hotel room that evening, his privacy was suddenly invaded by some Indian fans. 'Underwood! Underwood!' was all they cried as they directed their camera at him and clicked. After ordering them out of his room, he later came down to the hotel foyer only then to be greeted by the happy group of photographers who asked him to sign the photo of him in the bath.

Still in an era when official receptions were a staple part of touring, he flew the flag better than most. Room-mate Pocock later wrote, 'Underwood was a strange man in that he grew old before his time. He always had a supply of small talk, which made him a great asset at obligatory cocktail parties. We would wind him up, point out the Governor General, wife and friend and he would natter away quite happily for an hour or so. And when the party was over, they would all agree that they had just met an extremely pleasant young man. They were right of course since he was one of the nicest men who ever played Test cricket, but in the early years he was an earnest, intense, line and length companion. Over the past few years his interests have widened, and greater confidence has brought through a sense of humour he never knew he possesses.'

With only one wicket in the first two games, critics speculated whether Underwood merited inclusion in the Test team, but, as Woodcock noted, he'd claimed only one victim in the first two matches on the previous tour to Australia and yet only Snow exceeded his tally of wickets in the Tests. Knowing how well suited he was by the protracted tempo of five-day cricket, Woodcock remained hopeful that he would thrive in the Tests.

His faith in him was amply vindicated in the first Test at Delhi, memorably won by England. With the two sides evenly matched after the first innings, Underwood struck at the heart of the Indian innings by removing Gavaskar, Sardesai, Viswanath and Engineer, the latter after he'd revived his side's hopes with a swashbuckling 63. (Recalling him as one of the fairest opponents to play against, Engineer said that he was the first to applaud a good shot.)

Set 201 to win, England faltered at first but an unbeaten 70 from captain Lewis eased them to a six-wicket victory on Christmas Day. Underwood never forgot the joy of that win as they celebrated with an open-top bus ride through the streets of Delhi, waving to bemused passers-by, and drinks at the British Consulate, where they sang carols rather badly.

Buoyed by their unexpected success, England approached the Calcutta Test with renewed confidence. Daily crowds of 70,000 added colour to another riveting contest with the outcome remaining in doubt to the last. In a low-scoring game Underwood played his part by dismissing Engineer twice and Gavaskar, but for all the endeavours of the England bowlers their batsmen succumbed to the genius of Bishan Bedi and Chandrasekhar to lose by 28 runs.

With the series tied at 1-1, Underwood's withdrawal from the third Test at Madras because of sunstroke, sustained from excessive sunbathing, proved critical given the turning pitch. India won by four wickets and following draws at Bangalore and Bombay in the final two games they won the series 2-1. One man pivotal to their success was their flamboyant all-rounder Salim Durani, who could excite any crowd with his spectacular hitting. At Calcutta he responded to a roar from one of the stands to hit a six by striking Underwood in their direction a few balls later; then at Bombay he enlivened proceedings by plundering him for 18 runs off four balls. Recalling his exploits later, he wrote, 'In fact, it was against Tony Lewis's English team when batting against Norman Gifford or the left-armer Derek Underwood that I batted with ease and lofted their ball to get some fresh air in the sky.'

Subjected to Durani's withering assault, Underwood gained some revenge by snaring Gavaskar and Engineer in the second innings, the former for the fourth time in the series and the latter for the fifth. (A large number of his 297 victims were top-order batsmen.) 'The performance of the England spinners, Derek Underwood and Pat Pocock, were harder to evaluate,' commented *Wisden*. 'They did not often bowl badly, although by now it must be accepted that Underwood's menace lessens once he leaves England, yet they seldom threatened to win a Test match. By modern standards they performed creditably, but they were constantly put at a disadvantage by being seen in company with the Indian spinners.'

From India, MCC moved on to Pakistan to play a further three Tests on flat wickets against the full might of Majid, Mushtaq, Asif and Zaheer. In the first Test at Lahore, Underwood was England's best bowler, but his 0-119 in the second Test at Hyderabad cost him his place in favour of off-spinner Jack Birkenshaw. Never happy when omitted, he respected Lewis's explanation that the pitch was more suited to Birkenshaw and that Gifford was bowling well. The captain's judgement proved vindicated by events. Both slow bowlers took five wickets in Pakistan's second innings, giving England an outside chance of victory before their lower order saw them to safety.

With Illingworth back in charge for the home series against New Zealand that summer Gifford kept his place in the first two games, but his lack of success brought his Test career to an end. Underwood returned for the third Test against New Zealand and played in all three games against West Indies. Up against a formidable batting line-up, including a slew of left-handers such as Roy Fredericks, Alvin Kallicharran, Clive Lloyd and Sobers, he posed few terrors, not least in the final Test at Lord's, where

England suffered a crushing defeat. That game signalled the end of Illingworth's reign as captain following a record of 12 wins and five losses in his 31 games in charge, with Underwood being the match-winner in many of those games. He was replaced by Kent captain Mike Denness.

Throughout Underwood's career cricket was at the centre of his universe and he relied a lot on his family to help him cope with more worldly demands. Living at home until his marriage, aged 28, he was spared domestic chores and found his parents a receptive audience in the many discussions about his performance. Intensely proud of him, they ensured that nothing stood in the way of his destiny and followed him all over the world, not least to Sydney where England regained the Ashes in 1971.

Popular with Derek's team-mates, Leslie and Evelyn were a constant fixture at Kent home games and readily provided the broadcaster Brian Johnston with a cup of tea and a bun whenever he joined them at their car. Their only embarrassing moment came at Southampton in May 1964 when Rustler, their beloved Airedale, raced on to the playing area and held up play for several minutes while he cavorted with another dog. The interruption appeared to unsettle Hampshire opener Roy Marshall, who was out two balls later.

Brian Luckhurst once remarked that the only man his own wife would leave him for was Underwood. It was meant in jest but illustrated Underwood's appeal to women. Even those with no interest in cricket could be captivated by his charm and civility. During his 20s he courted several air hostesses before meeting Dawn Sullivan, a vivacious, no-nonsense receptionist then living and working in London. Born in Leeds, the eldest daughter of

Gerry and Day Sullivan, her family had moved to Cliftonville, a suburb of Margate, in 1961 where they ran a small guest house in Northdown Road for the rest of the decade. There she and her sister Gail made a name for themselves in Lido competitions, swooping up many a prize. As the winner was often judged by the loudest appreciation of the audience, Day would clap wildly for her daughters. Crowned Margate's Carnival Queen in 1962 and Miss Deal in 1963, Dawn was also runner-up to Miss Wales in 1966, an accomplishment that won her an all-expenses trip to Long Beach, California, the following year to represent Wales in the Miss International Beauty Congress.

A keen sportswoman, who'd been close to Kent's Stuart Leary, she'd met Underwood through her good friend Sue Ealham, the wife of Alan Ealham, and saw him play for the first time at Headingley in 1972 when he took ten wickets against Australia.

Becoming engaged in May 1973, they married that October at King Edward's School, Witley (where Dawn's father now worked as the beadle), followed by a reception at the Georgian Hotel, Haslemere. Keith Underwood was best man and Mark and Louisa Ealham acted as attendants.

With Underwood due to tour West Indies early in the new year, it was he who stayed at home while Dawn went out to work, but his domestic and practical skills fell far short of his cricketing ones, a deficiency that improved little with age.

More concerning was his overwrought temperament which he inherited from his mother. Conscientious to a fault in his public duties and very sensitive to public opinion, he could be high-maintenance in private. And that was before anyone had ever heard of Kerry Packer.

Chapter 5

The Quiet Assassin

PERHAPS THE great paradox of Underwood's career was how such a gentle, diffident personality off the field should be such a demon on it. According to the Middlesex and England fast bowler Mike Selvey, he was the most single-minded, dedicated bowler he'd ever seen, and when the author Christopher Sandford described Underwood in his book *Laker and Lock: The Odd Couple* as the archetypal 'nice guy', who hated most of his opponents while on the field, Underwood promptly rang him to complain. 'It should have been all his opponents,' he said.

With his boyish face and his unathletic gait, Underwood looked far removed from the profile of a sporting icon. Somerset off-spinner Vic Marks wrote: 'However you viewed him, he was unusual, an ordinary, innocent-looking cricketer; minus the rippling muscles or gleaming swagger of the superstar international, who would not look out of place in club cricket in the shires on a Saturday afternoon.' Blessed with a very strong back, shoulders and legs, he expressed surprise when people described him as frail. 'Stamina is needed above all for a bowler like me. I might have to bowl for two or two-and-a-half hours,' he commented. 'He has hardly ever missed a match,' wrote Knott. 'I remember once after he had been bowling at

Bournemouth non-stop through an innings, Hampshire's Nigel Cowley came into the dressing room and said, "I wish I had your legs." The wonderful thing about him which goes unnoticed is his supreme cricket fitness. He is one of the old school who always believes that to get fit for bowling you bowl and bowl, whether in the middle or in the nets, although he much prefers the middle.'

'There is one thing you can always guarantee with Derek and that is his keenness and enthusiasm to bowl for us,' commented his county captain Alan Ealham on him reaching 100 wickets for the season in 1978. When Ealham said to him, 'Deadly, you can warm up,' he would twitch his finger and reply, 'I'm ready.' Even on a boiling hot day and the flattest of pitches, he still loved to bowl.

So absorbed was he by his bowling that he didn't like setting his field (although he favoured an orthodox run-saving one in addition to two or three up close). Mark Nicholas, captaining him in the 1985 MCC–Australians fixture, was astonished by his indifference. 'Up to you, matey,' he said with a smile. 'You're captain. I'll go with whatever you think.' Calling himself a low-mentality bowler reluctant to experiment, he wheeled away over after over on a flat wicket, waiting for the batsmen to self-destruct. While he celebrated a dismissal with a clap or a raised fist, his face would etch with mortification if he bowled a bad ball or pained resignation if luck went against him. When Greig missed a sitter off him in the Bombay Test of 1972/73, he exclaimed through gritted teeth to captain Tony Lewis, 'That was cruel, cruel,' a remark with which Lewis always greeted him thereafter. Stephen Brenkley, *The Independent*'s cricket correspondent for many years, recalls how, when covering a game between Oxford

University and Kent in 1981, he was pressed into action as an emergency fielder for the latter to compensate for the absence of a couple of their players following a late night out on the town. Placed at mid-on, it wasn't long before Oxford's Nick Mallett, later a renowned South African rugby coach, launched a big hit against Underwood. The ball went swirling up in the air and Brenkley dropped it. He immediately apologised to Underwood, who replied, 'Okay, concentrate next time.'

According to Trevor Bailey, Underwood, like fellow left-armers Wilfred Rhodes and Hedley Verity, acquired all the subtleties including flight, change of pace and the arm ball, but unlike the others his pace was medium, his trajectory flatter and his break owed more to cut than spin. In the opinion of Knott, his additional speed compared to a normal spinner was his greatest asset. 'If only the occasional delivery moves it deviates so quickly that it can have any batsman in trouble – it only needs one ball to go like that and the batsman feels that he must play slightly outside the line.'

Trudging thoughtfully back to his mark, he glided up to the crease, some ten paces – his run-up obscured by the umpire – to deliver with a classical sideways-on action, making full use of his body, obtaining maximum height of arm and a full follow-through. Employing a longer delivery stride than most slow bowlers, which explains why he was no-balled so often, his front foot landed wide, bisecting the popping and return creases. He also used the width of the crease to vary the angle and get more cut and spin on the ball.

Neither an orthodox spinner nor cutter, he gripped the ball in the same way as the orthodox slow armer, although he didn't have to rely on such violent finger and wrist movement to make it turn – hence his absence of sore fingers – gaining deviation by dragging his bowling hand across the ball as his arm came over. While his lack of movement served him well on wet pitches compared to Tony Lock, who turned it too much on those surfaces, his lower trajectory meant that he didn't achieve the same turn and bounce on flat pitches as a more orthodox spinner.

Amid his many attributes what really defined Underwood was his complete mastery on a rain-affected pitch, when he would drive the ball into the pitch and take out divots. Les Ames regarded him as the greatest bowler on a damp pitch that he'd ever seen. As someone who loved to go down the wicket to the slower ball, he admitted that 'I could never have done it against Derek. I'd have been dead if I tried.'

'If you got on a crumbling pitch, nine times out of ten Deadly would win you the game,' commented Keith Fletcher. 'You could argue whether he was a genuine spinner or a medium-pacer, but on dusty and damp pitches Underwood was the best I played,' wrote Brian Luckhurst. 'There have been many times when fielding either at short leg or gully that I could not see how the batter was going to survive let alone score some runs. They have tried all ways, playing forward, playing back and even in desperation charging up the wicket. But the result was normally the same one, a walk back to the pavilion.'

Reliving the ordeal of facing him, Hampshire batsman Mark Nicholas wrote, 'You'd hear the ball spinning like a top. It was a kind of magical beauty in its performance, brutal in its effect and irresistible in its result.' 'I do not know anybody who could play him or hit him after it had rained on those pitches,' recalled Boycott. 'Once it had rained, he was unplayable because he bowled at a slightly quicker pace than the orthodox left-armer. Derek did not spin the ball so much as cut it and because he was faster and flatter than most slow bowlers, he was on to you and making you hurry any stroke.'

Ironically, it was Boycott with his immaculate technique that came closest to combating Underwood in these conditions, as the latter recounted: 'On a wicket where the ball was really gripping, I'd bowl to him and somehow it didn't seem to turn at all. That's how good he was. I'd only realise that the ball was really turning when Boycs took a single. Then I was bowling at someone else and suddenly I'd be beating the bat twice an over.'

Boycott thought that compared to some bowlers who buckled under the weight of expectation Underwood thrived on the opportunity to bowl a side out, an opinion Underwood disputed. He wrote, 'Whenever there was rain about, the lads used to say, "Oh, we'll be okay, we've got Deadly," but that was pressure on me, even though it was meant as a compliment.'

It was Underwood's good fortune that he was well supported by a cordon of highly skilled close-in fielders such as Cowdrey at slip, Luckhurst at leg slip and Leary at short leg and the brilliance of Knott behind the stumps. Ever since playing for Kent Schools together, they remained highly committed to their craft, practising assiduously and blending in seamlessly with their team-mates. Neither would be found bad-mouthing them any more than they would abuse their opponents in the middle. Probably the most derogatory comment either of them ever made was Knott's aside to Hampshire batsman Andrew Murtagh when he was floundering against Underwood. 'Don't worry, mate,' he said. 'He's made better batsmen than you look stupid.'

Modest, unassuming and highly appreciative of each other's unique talent, they were two of a kind, both supremely competitive – Underwood loathed being beaten by Knott at table tennis when young – yet for all their similarities, there were subtle differences. Whereas Underwood enjoyed the camaraderie of the bar and entertained lavishly, Knott was essentially a loner who now lives quietly in Cyprus unrecognised by the expat community and whose austere lifestyle and rigorous fitness regime helped make him a genius.

He was also a more confident, unflappable personality who, unlike Underwood, didn't follow the crowd, rarely read the press and wasn't beholden to his critics. Quietly opinionated and left-wing, a rarity in the world of cricket, he resented being omitted from the first three Tests of the West Indies tour of 1967/68 and held captain Colin Cowdrey culpable, not least his failure to explain the decision. Never a great apologist for his style of captaincy, he preferred playing under Denness, admiring his enthusiasm for the one-day game and his coolness under pressure. Underwood, in contrast, a *Telegraph*-reading Conservative, remained close to Cowdrey and preferred his collegiate style of leadership to Denness's more remote approach, especially when liaising with his bowlers.

An astute reader of the game, Knott was invaluable in discerning the pace of the wicket, dissecting a batsman's technique or reassuring his team-mate when he became flustered. One of the very few occasions he did disconcert him came in net practice at Canterbury one day, when he anticipated the kind of delivery Underwood would bowl, something he could tell from examining his posture. 'He was just about to run up and bowl and I shouted out "seamer, you're going to bowl a seamer",' Knott recalled. 'He bowled the delivery, then a few balls later I said, "slow ball" and he got very annoyed, saying, "You can't possibly know what I'm going to bowl."

'We finished the net but I'd made him think. He said, "If you can tell what I'm going to bowl, after all these years of playing cricket, batsmen around the county circuit will get to know as well. I must do something about it."

'He then started putting the umpire in the line of his run-up so that the batsman couldn't see him approaching. He'd then pop out at the last moment from behind the umpire to send down the delivery. Deadly became even more deadly after that.'

In the middle they formed a telepathic understanding so that Knott could send a discreet signal indicating what type of delivery he should bowl. If he looked skywards when he was running in, the ball would be tossed up and if downward it would be speared in. Another ploy was for Underwood to bowl just outside the left-hander's leg stump in the hope that he would overbalance and be stumped. One year this brought several victims although not Leicestershire's Jack Birkenshaw, who was missed twice in one over by Knott.

Inevitably Knott's prime value was on rain-affected pitches when Underwood was at his most venomous, gathering the ball effortlessly as it flew everywhere. Recalling the scene Henry Blofeld wrote, 'In drying conditions, Underwood made the ball do everything but talk. From a good length, the ball would fly past the batsman's face or turn miles, lifting sharply at the same time, or maybe skid through low past leg stump. Yet every ball that passed invariably found the middle of Knott's gloves. If a catch or stumping came his way, it was not wasted. At times it was like an Olympian gymnast at the peak of his form.' Such was his immaculate keeping to Underwood on the unpredictable pitch at Headingley in 1972 that even the Australians were left astounded at his prowess. 'We watched in disbelief,' recalled Ian Chappell. 'The ball leapt or it squatted, and Knotty never missed one.'

'What a comfort it has been for me to know that day in and day out I have been bowling with the world's best wicketkeeper at the other end to take advantage of any error I may cause the batsman to make,' commented Underwood. Together they accounted for 198 victims.

Underwood also had the skill and mentality to succeed on all surfaces. Boycott wrote, 'People always talk about him on a wet pitch because he was so lethal on those. But he would bowl you out on a dry one because he was so accurate.' Adhering to Australian leg-spinner Bill O'Reilly's dictum for spinners, 'Give them nothing,' Underwood built pressure on batsmen and did not give them loose balls. 'Even on good wickets he never got slogged,' noted Yorkshire and England batsman John Hampshire. 'The thing about Deadly is that he never seemed to bowl a bad ball,' concurred Barry Richards. According to Jim Laker, his accuracy was as consistent as anything he'd seen.

Underwood's inclination for frugality was drummed into him by Colin Cowdrey. 'If I suddenly bowled a slower ball and the batsman leant back and hit it for four, Colin would walk down the wicket with his hands on his hips as if to say, "Oh God, what did you do that for?" he wrote. 'Derek loved bowling,' recalled Alan Dixon. 'He took it as a personal affront if anyone scored off him, especially if it put a left-hander on strike.' 'If you were a fielder and not on your toes, maybe nodding off a bit, and you allowed the batsman to sneak a quick single,' wrote Boycott, 'he would never say anything, but you could tell he was cross.'

Andrew Hignell, scorer for Glamorgan in the early 1980s, recalled the demeanour of Claude Lewis, his Kent counterpart, to Underwood. 'His eyes would light up as Derek bowled maiden after maiden. In those days, we used scorebooks with rows, each of ten overs. Claude took great delight in telling me how many times Derek had completed an entire row of maiden overs with no runs being scored from 60 consecutive balls. During the first interval of a game the scorer always brought in the bowlers' analyses to the Kent dressing room at lunchtime and Underwood, tongue in cheek, would say, "How could they get three off me? They're nicking me out of the game."'

'Derek was the most miserly bowler I've ever seen,' commented John Shepherd. 'Even in benefit matches he hated being hit.' According to England team-mate Bob Willis, he would bowl maiden after maiden and would get very frustrated if other bowlers weren't interested in doing the same. He would never resort to Bishan Bedi's approach of buying wickets, like he did against England at Lord's in 1974 when he finished with figures of 6-226. 'If I had been bowling it would have hurt me to have seen the batsmen take singles off me when and how they pleased,' he wrote in *Beating the Bat*. 'I believe it is far more important to try to hold the batsman.'

Shepherd recalled how he and Asif used to stand at mid-on and mid-off respectively to his bowling and encourage him to give the ball some air. If the batsman hit it back over his head for four, Underwood would put his hand to his head and say, 'Why did you make me do that?' Any setback could unsettle him and lead to fraught discussions back home that evening.

Aside from his metronomic accuracy, which even contained rampant hitters such as Colin Milburn and Farokh Engineer,

Underwood tended to beat batsmen on a good pitch by change of pace or a very effective arm ball, the legacy of his days as a seamer. Somerset all-rounder Vic Marks found facing him a daunting experience. He wrote, 'Once in 1976 I impishly late-cut him for four and Underwood said nothing. He never did. He was far too decent to contemplate sledging a batsman. But my batting partner, Brian Rose, spoke up. "Whatever you do, don't try that again," he said. I may have nodded but a couple of overs later I was tempted to try another cut; this time the ball was his deadly inswinger, which was about 10mph quicker and the stumps were splintered before my cut was complete. The bails flew high like Rose's eyebrows.'

Gradually Underwood became better at adapting his style to different pitches, bowling a little slower on drier ones, never better seen than in India in 1976/77. Reflecting on his numerous dismissals by Underwood, Gavaskar recalled how Underwood had deceived him in flight and had him playing too early. At Old Trafford in 1974, he bowled Viswanath with a beauty that pitched on leg and knocked out the off stump.

Ian and Greg Chappell, who hated being hemmed in by Underwood's close fielders, tried hard to exploit what the cricket writer Christopher Martin-Jenkins called the one great flaw in his character, his tendency to get too easily demoralised when batsmen scored freely off him. Ian Chappell noted how aggrieved he became at being swept from outside the off stump during his two centuries at the Oval in 1972 and 1975. When Chappell came out of retirement to play in WSC, Underwood said to him, 'That bloody broom [alluding to the sweep]. I thought I'd seen the last of it.'

'Underwood is the sort of bowler a batsman plays into form if he concentrates purely on defence,' commented Greg

Chappell. If the batsman allowed him to bowl a good line, he would eventually dismiss him. 'But if you attack Underwood early in his bowling session, it can affect his line and thinking and lead to his removal from the attack.'

One student of that philosophy was Ted Dexter, who never rated Underwood and once had to apologise for saying this publicly. Over the years he had much the better of their duels, with centuries against him in 1963 and 1964 prior to his double century at Hastings in 1968, so much so that Underwood disliked bowling to him. (Although he regretted his absence when he took 9-28 against Sussex in 1964.)

Another batsman who won his spurs against him was Brian Davison, the hard-hitting Rhodesian who played for Leicestershire. Not only did he bludgeon him off the front foot; he also stepped back outside the leg stump to hit him through the off side.

A more studious response came from Zaheer Abbas, one of Pakistan's finest batsmen. During a post-match discussion after scoring runs off him, he disconcerted Underwood by saying how much he enjoyed facing his bowling, but far from slighting him it was meant as a compliment, since it forced him to concentrate harder. Underwood certainly brought the best out of him because in 1971 he made 138 for Pakistan against Kent on a difficult pitch at Gravesend before stroking his way to a peerless 274 in the first Test at Edgbaston; then at Canterbury in 1976 he ruined Knott's benefit match by running Kent ragged with scores of 230 not out and 104 not out and reducing Underwood to mere mortality, his one wicket in the game costing 140 runs.

Left-handers with their ability to hit with the spin were a particular bane. Alan Dixon was captain of Kent against

Northamptonshire at Wellingborough in 1968 when Underwood came off second best to South African Hylton Ackerman. In the tightest of games which Kent won by five runs, they'd been seriously incapacitated by an injury to fast bowler John Dye, who aggravated an old hamstring injury by knocking around with a football. Consequently, he lasted only four balls, forcing his good friend Alan Brown to field for the rest of the game and leaving Dixon with fewer bowling options.

At first all went according to plan as Northamptonshire lost early wickets until they rallied under Ackerman. 'He had such strong forearms,' recalled Dixon. 'He wasn't frightened to hit the ball in the air. He picked Derek up and kept wafting him wide of mid-on. And at that stage of his career Derek found it very difficult to bowl to anybody who did that.' Consequently, Dixon took him off and didn't bowl him again until Ackerman was out; then in their second innings when they required 125 to win, he made ten bowling changes in the hour after lunch when Ackerman was in to try and shield Underwood from him, a ploy which very much succeeded. Shepherd's dismissal of him for 35 proved the defining moment in the game, as he and Underwood bowled Kent to victory. Not that it proved much of a consolation for Brown, since it was Dye rather than him that picked up the winning bonus.

Sobers thought that on a good pitch he could get after Underwood, figuring that the ball hardly turned. Playing for Nottinghamshire at Dover in 1968 and riled that Kent hadn't declared, he took his ire out on their attack, hitting Underwood for three sixes and scoring the fastest century of the season; similarly, during his imperious 150 not out for West Indies against England at Lord's in 1973 he treated Underwood with disdain. Rating Sobers the finest player he ever encountered, Underwood wrote, 'When Gary was on form, I don't think there was any bowler who could hope to keep him quiet. He had every stroke and was equally strong off front and back foot.'

Clive Lloyd was another West Indian whose attacking instincts reaped their reward, most notably his 163 for Lancashire against Kent at Dartford in 1970. Underwood thought he had the ball to get him, since he detected a weakness when playing for Derrick Robins' XI against the West Indians the previous year. Every time the ball soared out of the ground Shepherd asked a baffled Underwood if that was the ball.

Other left-handers who had their moments included West Indies opener Roy Fredericks and South Africa's Lee Irvine who played for Essex in the early 1970s, but in 25 years the roll call of those who dominated him was strictly limited.

Despite entreaties by coaches, selectors and critics to turn himself into a more orthodox left-arm spinner like Hedley Verity, Underwood was loath to forsake the method that had served him so well over the years. He wrote in *Beating the Bat*, 'To change my style of bowling would also require me to change my whole approach to bowling from a mental point of view. I'm a mean bowler rather in the mould of Illingworth. I hate every run that is scored off me. I don't like trying to buy my wickets – that is just not the way I play the game.

'Whenever I hear the argument put forward that I should slow down and be more of a flight bowler there is one other point I take into consideration. Just how many flight bowlers are there in top international cricket today? Very, very few.'

He even went to some length to dissect Verity's bowling statistics, pointing out that he'd taken 144 wickets in 40 Tests, whereas he had reached that figure in four fewer Tests and by bowling far fewer overs. Turning to their records in Australia, he claimed that Verity's tally of 21 wickets (average 34.57) on two tours there in 1932/33 and 1936/37 was inferior to his tally of 33 in 1970/71 and 1974/75 (the comparison was made before his tour there in 1979/80), but then Verity was squaring up to Don Bradman in his prime, a man he dismissed eight times in Tests, more than any other bowler.

Less classical was Underwood's batting, a part of the game which he greatly enjoyed, especially when it really mattered. A prolific run-scorer in his youth, he was recommended to Kent as a batsman by Tony Lock and he displayed enough promise to impress Les Ames at his trial. John Shepherd, on arrival from Barbados in 1965, recalls seeing him playing all the shots at pre-season practice in the indoor school and thinking he looked the best batsman on view, and no less an authority than Colin Cowdrey predicted that he could turn into a genuine all-rounder (although his batting average in his early years hardly suggested this). That this didn't occur owed something to Kent's strength in batting, Underwood's growing prominence as a bowler and to his technical limitations. A gritty tail-ender, he thrived on the challenge of acting as nightwatchman, knowing the opportunity it presented of being able to build an innings on the morrow and it is no coincidence that his most notable innings were played in that role: his memorable century against Sussex at Hastings in 1984 and a rather fortunate 80 against Lancashire at Old Trafford in 1969, as one local report made clear. 'To be truthful, he didn't look notably a better batsman when he was out than when he went in, but Lancashire could neither beat his defensive prod, nor hold the ball when he offered a chance.'

He also made two of his three highest Test scores as nightwatchman: 43 against Pakistan at the Oval in 1974 when he put on 129 for the second wicket with Dennis Amiss – 'He batted with all the decorum of a Test opener and left the shots to Amiss,' pronounced *The Observer* – and 43 against Australia in rather more testing circumstances at Sydney in 1979/80. On the 13 occasions he performed this role for England he occupied the crease for an average of 43 minutes.

Renowned for his forward prod and gentle push into the off side, he scored the bulk of his runs with a squirt through gully or, more likely, a short-arm jab over square leg, particularly effective in the limited-overs game. Occasionally something more refined would appear, John Woodcock once remarking that one Underwood cover-driven boundary reminded him of Dexter in his pomp.

Always courageous at the best of times, Underwood would endeavour to get into line against the pacemen, but he couldn't pick up the short ball quickly enough or learn to sway out of the way. According to D'Oliveira, who batted with him on his Test debut, he lacked the technical expertise to defend himself, a deficiency that probably accounted for Boycott's tart observation that he 'couldn't bat for toffee'. To be fair to Boycott, his view was supported by Keith Fletcher who ranked Underwood as a genuine number 11, suspect to a yorker from John Lever. Yet, for all his travails against the short ball when facing the likes of Dennis Lillee, Jeff Thomson and Michael Holding, he continued to sell his wicket dearly and make the most of his limited ability to the benefit of Kent and England.

Although no thoroughbred in the field with his splayed feet, Underwood was a reliable mid-on or long leg who chased hard and had a safe pair of hands, not least off his own bowling. During his career he recorded 107 dismissals in this manner, one of the finest being the return catch he took off the West Indian Charlie Davis at Headingley in 1969 when he flung himself to his left to grab the ball one-handed just before it touched the ground. As with all aspects of his game, he gave his all to his fielding and even in later years he would keep the local launderette in business with his flying dives around the boundary to stop a run.

It was this career-long commitment that helped make him the player he was, and a team-mate admired by all.

Chapter 6

Hard Pounding

FOLLOWING ILLINGWORTH'S dethronement, the man chosen to lead MCC in West Indies was Mike Denness. Vice-captain to Lewis in India and Pakistan the previous winter, Denness had struggled with the bat, so much so that he hadn't played under Illingworth the following summer. Somewhat aloof, especially with his bowlers, and still short of runs, he lacked the personality to unite his England team-mates, not least Geoff Boycott, who opposed his leadership at every stage.

After a series of draws in the provincial games, England approached the first Test at Port-of-Spain very much as underdogs and, true to form, they lost by seven wickets, but the match will always be remembered for a notorious incident at the end of the second day. Underwood bowled the last ball of the final over to his Kent team-mate Bernard Julien, who played it defensively past Greig fielding at silly point. As Greig ran after it, Knott uprooted the stumps and Kallicharran, at the non-striker's end, started walking down the wicket towards the pavilion.

Greig by now had retrieved the ball and, seeing Kallicharran out of his ground, he threw down the non-striker's wicket. He appealed and umpire Douglas Sang Hue, who hadn't called time, felt compelled to give him out. The dismissal, which appeared to breach the spirit of the game, sparked uproar as Kallicharran stomped furiously back to the pavilion with 142 to his name. As an angry crowd gathered outside the ground, an emergency meeting was convened between the respective officials, captains and umpires and after hours of discussion it was agreed that Kallicharran should be reinstated.

The decision was met with some reluctance by the England team. 'The umpire hadn't called close of play, so he was out, no doubt about that,' Underwood told Greig's biographer David Tossell. 'For the sake of goodwill, it had to be changed, and the players accepted the ruling, but Kalli was at fault. He knows the rules, stay in the crease until the umpire calls close of play.'

Defeated in the first Test, England were again floundering in the second Test at Kingston when they began their second innings 230 runs behind with ten hours left. Amiss, a centurion in the first Test, again reached three figures but England looked doomed at 217/5 when Underwood joined him as nightwatchman. Feeling physically and mentally drained from a day in the heat, Amiss immediately asked him to take as much of the bowling as possible, which he did.

Told by Knott the next morning that he had to bat all day, Amiss walked to the middle with Underwood in eerie silence despite a capacity crowd anticipating another Roman triumph. Still 12 runs behind West Indies, Underwood had to endure seven overs of spin hemmed in by close fielders, which he never liked, then having survived the dexterity of Lance Gibbs he had to contend with the fearsome proposition of Keith Boyce bowling short with the new ball but, on this most placid of surfaces, he got into line and fended off everything. According to Christopher

Martin-Jenkins, he 'played like a suspicious bomb disposal officer putting a tentative bat towards the ball and then withdrawing swiftly as if he thought it would explode'. Once he walked down the pitch and asked Amiss, 'How am I doing?' 'Very well,' Amiss said. 'Better than myself.' 'Oh, am I really?' he answered and walked back looking very pleased. According to the Jamaica *Daily Gleaner*, 'he batted very much according to the textbook. He is seldom an easy wicket to get when it really matters.'

After 90 minutes of resistance Sobers had him caught behind, but his gritty effort inspired his team-mates to do likewise. Thanks to a memorable 262 not out from Amiss and invaluable support from Pat Pocock, Geoff Arnold and Bob Willis, they survived against all predictions to fight another day.

Omitted for the Barbados Test because of his lack of wickets, Underwood looked to the game against Guyana to regain his form, but he, along with Arnold, ran into trouble with the local umpires. According to Martin-Jenkins, 'Poor old Deadly, for whom cricket at the best of times is an earnest trouble against inscrutable fate, almost literally burst with indignation as time and again he beat the bat, hit the pad, but failed to get an affirmative response from the umpires.' In addition to having numerous lbw appeals turned down, Underwood was also repeatedly no-balled. Such was his frustration that on one occasion he snatched his sunhat from umpire Cec Kippins, who retaliated the following over by ostentatiously chucking back his sunhat.

Underwood and Arnold's dissent earned them a rebuke in the *Evening Post* of Guyana and other local journals. Commenting on some of the more outlandish articles about English boorishness, Martin-Jenkins, wrote, 'The fact remains, however, that whether the umpires were right or wrong neither Arnold nor Underwood achieved anything by losing their cool. Pompous moral principles aside, one of the first things one learns in cricket is that it is better to make the umpire one's friend rather than one's enemy.'

Sympathetic to Underwood's labours on these unresponsive pitches, Woodcock nevertheless suggested he could learn from Birkenshaw's success against Guyana by his willingness to give the ball some air. 'This is something that Underwood can seldom bring himself to do. Today, on one of the few occasions that he tossed up something tempting, he bowled Blair.'

Restored to the side for the Guyana Test, Underwood had little chance to shine because the game was ruined by the weather, but the opportunity to dismiss Kanhai with a beauty in the closing stages – one of the best balls he'd ever bowled – brought about a leap of joy.

After draws in Barbados and Guyana, everything hinged on the final Test back at Port-of-Spain. Two epic innings from Boycott and exceptional bowling from Greig, who extracted turn and bounce with his fast off-breaks, kept England in the game. Beginning the last day at 30/0 in pursuit of a target of 226, West Indies openers Roy Fredericks and Lawrence Rowe proceeded carefully to 63, whereupon five wickets fell for 22 runs as Greig once again took charge. A sixth-wicket stand of 50 between Sobers and Deryck Murray restored West Indian hopes until Sobers, frustrated by Underwood's accuracy, hit over his slower ball and was bowled. While a dispirited Sobers retreated to the pavilion in what proved to be his final Test innings, a jubilant Underwood ran down the pitch to Knott, who seized him by the waist and lifted him off the ground. It proved the decisive moment in the match as West Indies, falling prey to the pressure, slumped to defeat by 26 runs. Recalling Greig's 5-70 in the second innings to give him match figures of 13-156, Underwood said that given the West Indian line-up of five left-handers, the role of the off-spinner was greater. Calling it one of those spells that happen once in a lifetime, he said, 'At Trinidad he just hit the right rhythm and pace, but after that he never knew what to do, or what to bowl, on any particular day or wicket.'

'I was bowling at the other end and not getting it off the straight at all. I got one wicket in the Test, and it happened to be Sobers in the second innings when, if he had got 50 instead of 20, it would have been game over.' According to Amiss, Underwood's tremendous accuracy – 15-7-19-1 – was crucial to their victory and Greig, appreciating that his confidence was low after an unproductive series, commended him for his supporting role, something which Underwood much appreciated.

England's victory to level the series was as unexpected as it was fortunate because for the most part they had been outplayed. Greig aside, the bowlers had looked innocuous and for Underwood it was his most unrewarding tour with five wickets in four Tests – although this included Sobers twice – at 62.80 and 12 wickets in all games at 47.75.

His famine continued in the 3-0 defeat over India at home because of limited opportunities, then in the first Test against Pakistan he dropped tail-ender Sarfraz Nawaz who went on to make 50 in a low-scoring game, but his luck more than changed at Lord's. Batting first on a firm pitch, Pakistan started auspiciously, reaching 51/0 before heavy rain intervened. When play resumed in brilliant sunshine, Denness bowled Underwood immediately and when the effect of the roller began to wear off, he carried all before him, disposing of Zaheer, Mushtaq and Asif Iqbal for a total of three runs between them. He also accounted for the left-handed Wasim Raja, who advanced down the wicket and struck him sweetly only to fall victim to a stupendous leaping catch by Greig in front of the sightscreen.

After England gained a lead of 140, Pakistan batted carefully in benign conditions to reach 173/3 at the close on Saturday. Their fightback, however, was once again blighted by the weather when a torrential downpour on Sunday night led to water seeping through the covers on to the pitch. Compelled to run the gauntlet yet again when play began on Monday evening, Pakistan's fourth-wicket pair, Mushtaq and Wasim Raja, added another 19 runs before Underwood, having swapped to over the wicket to exploit the rough, had Raja caught at short leg for 53 off a ball that turned and lifted. He then removed Asif, caught at point, Imran Khan, taken at short leg, and cleaned bowled Intikhab Alam, all without scoring, followed by Sarfraz Nawaz and Wasim Bari. In 11.5 overs he captured 6-9 to finish with 8-51 for the innings and match figures of 13-71.

While Pakistan manager Omar Kureishi issued a vigorous protest to MCC about the negligence of their covering, England stood on the cusp of victory before more rain on the final day prevented further play.

The controversy once again detracted from Underwood's performance, much to his chagrin. He wrote, 'Believe me, that Lord's wicket was not as difficult as their batsmen made it look. The majority of the batsmen surrendered more readily in the second innings than they should have done. I know I would have struggled to have bowled out most county sides at Lord's that day.'

Buoyed by an unbeaten summer, MCC prepared for Australia in confidence, unaware of the tornado that awaited them. It was a measure of Denness's limited authority that he couldn't persuade his fellow selectors to pick John Snow, a grievous blunder, or convince Boycott to end his self-imposed exile from Test cricket. (He'd withdrawn from the England team after the first Test against India that summer and later withdrew from the team to tour Australia having initially accepted.)

Unlike on his previous three tours, Underwood began well, taking seven wickets in the game against South Australia, guaranteeing selection for the first Test at Brisbane. Since the drawn series in England over two years earlier Ian Chappell's side had evolved into a world-class outfit, their dazzling out-cricket accompanied by a bristling aggression designed to intimidate their opponents. Leading the charge was the opening attack of Dennis Lillee and Jeff Thomson, a relative unknown who stunned his opponents by the ferocity of his pace and steep bounce. Entering at 168/7 in reply to Australia's first innings of 309, Underwood stood firm while Greig launched a thrilling counter-attack, irking Lillee by signalling his own boundaries. Recalling the occasion, Greig wrote, 'Later in that innings I was joined at the wicket by Derek Underwood, one of the bravest tail-enders I have ever seen. He came up to me for the customary mid-wicket chat and asked if I had any advice. "Yes," I replied. "Fight for your life." With a look that was half-amused and half-alarmed "Deadly" returned to the striker's end. His second ball from Thomson was a fearsome bouncer and "Deadly" took off in that often-photographed pose of his, both feet off the ground, head turned away and bat brandished in baseball fashion.

'As the ball soared under the elbow he had thrown in front of his face missing his ear by inches, Derek's placid expression turned into a look of horror. At the end of the over he came down the wicket and said simply, "I see what you mean."'

In response to Greig's inclination to continue to annoy Lillee, Underwood urged him to stop provoking the bowler. "Don't forget who is at the other end," I said. Greigy took no notice, which I did not think was very intelligent. You could be batting against Lillee at one minute to six and he would be breathing fire and calling you all the names under the sun. But at one minute past six he would be back in the dressing room and looking to share a can with you.'

Greig's stunning century and Underwood's 25 helped England to respectability, but their second innings proved even more unnerving when Lillee and Thomson made the ball rear alarmingly on a dangerously uneven pitch. Even tail-enders weren't spared the treatment, Thomson striking Underwood a painful blow on his hand. Observing his batting technique, Martin-Jenkins wrote, 'He made no attempt, generally speaking, to get behind the ball but he watched it like a hawk, and when he went for an attacking stroke he did so with all his might on the principle that if he edged the ball he would at least do so hard.'

Surviving for over an hour with Knott, he undid his good work after tea by slashing fatally at leg-spinner Terry Jenner, but as England subsided to a heavy defeat, he could derive some comfort from knowing that he was top scorer in the second innings with 30.

Originally down to play in the second Test at Perth, he was omitted on the morning of the match when the overcast weather persuaded the tour selectors to play an extra pace bowler. Despite the heroics of the 41-year-old Cowdrey, straight out of an English winter, Lillee and Thomson, supported by flawless close catching, once again proved too over-powering for the England batsmen. Outplayed, they salvaged a draw at the MCG when the Australians required just 55 from the final 15 (eight-ball) overs. Disgruntled by Underwood's field of six men on the leg side – there was an unwritten law in Australia that you could only have five on the leg side – the Australian batsmen made little effort to score off him, but they went on to the attack when Denness took the new ball. With two overs remaining and 14 required, the captain recalled Underwood. Martin-Jenkins wrote, 'Up to the wicket for the penultimate over came Mr Parsimonious himself, Derek Underwood, shoulders hunched, feet plodding out at an angle of 45 degrees, face red, grim and perspiring. Eight balls homed in on Lillee, each on his off stump, each half an inch short of a perfect length, each met with a straight defensive bat and a gesture of resignation. "Are you enjoying the tour?" I heard an Australian ask Underwood a few weeks later. "No," he replied, "it's all the bloody fielding." But in this one over the tightest slow bowler who ever wore an England cap earned most of his tour money.'

England's reprieve proved short-lived, since their heavy defeat at the SCG meant they surrendered the Ashes. The Adelaide Test saw the return of Denness, who'd dropped himself for the previous game because of loss of form. Winning the toss, he inserted Australia on a drying pitch and in conditions ideal for Underwood they slumped to 84/5. Ian Chappell recalled Ian Redpath battling away until he was incorrectly given out in the over before lunch caught by Greig at silly point off Underwood. 'An exasperated Redpath spat on his bat. The mirth of that moment did not detract from the fact that it had been an engaging sight to watch two highly competent players involved in such a herculean struggle.'

At this point Underwood had all five wickets, but Denness's failure to bowl off-spinner Fred Titmus in tandem at the other end proved a major blunder. Against a feckless pace attack, Doug Walters and Jenner mounted a spirited recovery and although Underwood ended up with 7-113 in the first innings it counted for little as the batsmen once again capitulated to Lillee and co. Defeat by 163 runs merely underlined the gulf between the two teams and even a consolation victory at the MCG did little to alter that perception.

For Underwood, who'd taken 11 of his 17 wickets at Adelaide, the tour had proved hard pounding, but according to *Wisden*, 'he bowled beautifully on all types of pitch, making cleverer use of flight than on previous tours, so that in effect he was often playing the part of an unorthodox slow left-hander. It reflected the quality of his bowling that of his 17 Test wickets, seven were Chappells – and not one a tail-ender.' Reflecting on the series, Underwood took aim at the raucous aggression of the crowds. 'They were delighted when anybody was hit and tried their hardest to work the bowlers up into a bouncer-pitching frenzy. As for the poor fielders, myself included, who fielded on the fence, the abuse we sometimes received had to be heard to be believed.'

After two Tests in New Zealand, Underwood returned home to an unusually hectic summer, since it was his benefit year. There were no hard and fast rules about who received a benefit, but it was customary at Kent, in line with many counties, to award one to players ten years after they received their county cap. The club allowed the beneficiary one collection per cricket week at home games and one collection at every Sunday game which took place in Kent. They also gave him the option of having a benefit match or a guarantee of £1,400 and Underwood chose the latter, given the vagaries of the weather.

That aside, the success of any benefit was largely down to the popularity of the beneficiary and his efforts to generate income. Not only was Underwood held in high esteem throughout the county, not least for his many appearances at club dinners and other charitable events, he was fortunate that Dawn gave up her job to work on his behalf. With cricket forming such a major part of their life, she found herself drawn into that universe, making friends with the other players' wives and enjoying listening to Kent supporters at matches discussing her husband's performance. She also attended various receptions in the hospitality marquees and cricket dinners at which her husband was speaking, the latter a taxing assignment, since she was often left to her own devices while he was introduced to all and sundry.

Underwood also relied greatly on his 13 local benefit committees which organised events such as bat raffles in pubs, golf days and dinner dances, but while extremely grateful to the club and their supporters for their generosity he did find the business of making money in this way rather degrading.

The year began with a glittering dinner at the Great Danes Hotel, near Maidstone, attended by 400 guests. Brian Johnston acted as master of ceremonies, football pundit Jimmy Hill and BBC sports presenter Frank Bough supervised the auction and Alec Bedser was the guest speaker. Just back from managing MCC in Australia where they'd been soundly beaten, Bedser dismissed allegations that the team had been riven by dissension, professing that he'd 'never known a happier lot of chaps: I had the utmost cooperation from all of them.'

He went on to praise Underwood for his dedication, team spirit and courage batting against Lillee and Thomson, an accolade that won him a standing ovation. Afterwards the Underwoods hosted Bedser for the night and Dawn remembers them counting the money from the auction on the drawing room carpet while Bedser slept soundly upstairs.

While Dawn took part in a fashion show at Canterbury, Underwood travelled to Glasgow to play for Keith's club, Poloc, in a benefit game, a gesture which he greatly appreciated, since it gave Scottish cricket a much-needed boost. Despite the massive amount of work required to organise a successful benefit, their efforts paid off, since it raised £24,118.

When England met Australia again that summer for a four-Test series after the inaugural World Cup, Underwood found little in the pitches to help him, and he rarely troubled the batsmen. A measly six-wicket tally was the sum result of his labours, but on bowling Marsh at Headingley he gained his 200th Test victim, the youngest Englishman to achieve this milestone.

With no official tour that winter, Underwood went to South Africa with the International Wanderers XI managed by Richie Benaud and captained by Greg Chappell. The side included John Shepherd, who had gone to South Africa with Derrick Robins' touring side in 1973, becoming the first black cricketer to play there, but at a time when the cricket authorities were trying to make the game more inclusive many of the old prejudices remained. One evening a group of players were out in a bar in Durban when Shepherd was refused service by the barman, an insult that greatly upset Underwood. Fellow tourist Mike Denness complained to Benaud, and the barman was sacked by the hotel management. On a lighter note, a diplomat at a cocktail party in Soweto welcomed the 'Australian' team to the city, at which point Ian Chappell went up to Underwood and said, 'Congratulations on finally representing a good team.' He wasn't amused.

With a strong bowling attack led by the Australians Lillee, Max Walker, Gary Gilmour and Ashley Mallett, Underwood's opportunities were limited in the three games against the South African Invitation XI, although his average was perfectly respectable and rather better than his performance when he returned with the England rebel side six years later.

Chapter 7

Gavaskar's Nemesis

ENGLAND'S HOME series against Australia in 1975 had brought about the demise of Denness after his ill-fated decision to insert his opponents in the first Test at Edgbaston. He was replaced by Tony Greig, who added a touch of spine to the England team. Encouraged by the progress made, he looked to seize the initiative against West Indies the following year with his notorious grovel comment, a statement that came back to haunt him all summer. In contrast to his bullish talk, he adopted an attritional approach, recalling veteran Brian Close, setting defensive fields and not bowling Underwood until 5.45pm on the opening day of the first Test, by which time Viv Richards was in total control. With a touch of genius, he stepped outside leg stump and lofted him high over extra cover for six before escaping a hard chance off him to Mike Hendrick at mid-off. By way of contrition, Greig opened with Underwood the next morning and although hit for another couple of sixes by Richards he gained some redress when the Antiguan holed out to Greig on the long-off boundary for a sublime 232. He then removed Kallicharran, Lloyd and Larry Gomes in the space of six overs, giving him overall figures of 4-82 in West Indies' formidable total of 482.

Richards' 232 and 63 had exposed the limitations of the England attack but a docile pitch helped them survive with a draw and at Lord's they took advantage of his absence to gain a 68-run lead on first innings. Having made a plucky 31 off Andy Roberts and Michael Holding, inviting the odd short one in the process, Underwood combined with Snow to bowl out West Indies for 182. According to *Wisden*, 'he rarely strayed off his immaculate length and line. Moreover, he varied his flight and acquired occasional turn.' Dismissing top scorers Gordon Greenidge for 84 and Clive Lloyd for 50, he then swept through the tail to finish with 5-39, his best figures against West Indies. In glorious weather, and with the Tavern in full voice, England returned to the pavilion to strains of 'Rule Britannia'. A washout the next day consigned the game to another draw but not before both sides had shown what they might have achieved with a touch more enterprise. In pursuit of a target of 323 in five hours, opener Roy Fredericks gave Underwood some stick, but he never suggested positive intent and when he and Lloyd were out in quick succession, the latter signalled the end of the run chase in the 14th of the final 20 overs. Greig, however with a touch of bravado, demanded they remain out there and with his team-mates huddled around the bat, Underwood bowled Bernard Julien and Larry Gomes before time ran out.

On a cracked, unpredictable surface at Old Trafford, West Indies batted first and made 211 (Underwood 3-55) before letting Roberts, Holding and Wayne Daniel loose on the England batsmen. A total of 71 was all they could manage, their travails summed up by the photo of a hapless Underwood, both feet off the ground, taking evasive action as a bouncer from Holding whistled by his head.

After Greenidge hit his second century of the match, the West Indian quicks went to town on openers John Edrich and Close with a spell of venomous short-pitched bowling, during which both were hit. While the England dressing room sat in stony silence Underwood opted out of the role of nightwatchman for the only time in his career, telling Greig that he was 'currently short of runs'. It was a message with which Greig sympathised, since he later admitted that that session had left him frightened for the only time in his career. As it was, both openers survived to stumps and, after a mauling in the Sunday papers, the West Indians, bowling a fuller length thereafter, duly reaped their reward. When Underwood was caught in the gully off Roberts, he completed yet another pair against West Indies.

Thrashed at Old Trafford and defeated at Headingley, England faced the cream of the West Indies batting on the most placid of wickets at the Oval. In broiling heat, the tourists won the toss and batted first. Although they lost Greenidge to Bob Willis for nought, Greig introduced Underwood into the attack after four overs, the beginning of two days' hard labour. Although more expensive than usual, he was unfortunate to have both Richards and Rowe dropped off him, the former a straightforward chance to Chris Balderstone, the latter a harder one to Knott. Led by Richards' 291, West Indies piled on the agony and by the time they declared at 687/8 on the second evening, Underwood had toiled away for 60.5 overs for figures of 3-165. Recalling Greig's boast that his team could outfield their opponents, opening bowler Mike Selvey said, 'When they were 600 for something and Deadly was standing there absolutely bedraggled after his 60th over, you looked around and you could see what he had out there. It was hardly a team of the greatest fielders. You just felt so sorry for Deadly.'

He did at least derive some pleasure from having Rowe stumped, Knott's 220th Test victim, enabling him to pass Godfrey Evans' record, a source of mutual delight as they hugged each other. 'It was lovely that it was off Derek Underwood,' Knott later commented. 'I had dropped quite a difficult catch so maybe it was meant to be that it was off Derek that I got the record.'

Reeling from a 3-0 loss and without a win in eight Tests under Greig, the selectors contemplated a change in captaincy for the subsequent tour of India. They ultimately kept faith with him, an act of loyalty well rewarded, since his leadership proved critical to England's series win, their first in India since Douglas Jardine led them in 1933/34.

A cult figure because of his showmanship on the previous tour, Greig used his charisma to win over the media, the umpires and crowds. He also forged an excellent team spirit with his dynamic leadership on the field, not least when they were struggling, and the great belief he placed in his players. This particularly applied to Underwood, who put his captaincy on a par with Brearley's. 'I could easily have been dropped [in the recent series against West Indies], but I played all the way through. He [Greig] would say, "Derek, you are number one on my list." That was Tony. I will never forget that and as a result performed better.'

Acknowledging that Underwood was vital to his winning strategy by plugging away at one end while the three quicks operated at the other, Greig rested him in the provincial games to keep him fresh for the Tests. On one occasion the two of them enjoyed a break at the tourist resort of Goa, where nude bathing was in fashion. 'We might as well join them, Deadly,' remarked Greig whipping off his shorts, but Underwood, modest as ever, declined to conform.

One of Underwood's room-mates was Yorkshire off-spinner Geoff Cope. He recalled, 'Derek and I had always been mates, and I kept ringing him: "What do I need?" He said, "Listen, you're going to be in charge of the Bovril. You need two big jars." I thought, is this a wind-up for the junior player? How do I play this? Every time I rang him, he would say, "Don't forget the Bovril."'

Assigned to share with Cope, Underwood would say to him intermittently, 'You've got the Bovril, haven't you?' And when Cope confirmed that he had, he would reply, 'Good, we don't need it yet. You keep it.'

It was on the way to Nagpur on the bus that Underwood turned to Cope and said, 'Today is the day for the Bovril. You've got it, haven't you?' 'We ended up in the army barracks where we had a board for a bed, one sheet, a pillow and a mosquito net,' Cope recalled, 'and the choice of six curries. So we got the Bovril out and had Bovril drinks.'

Cope had particular reason to be indebted to Underwood because of the compassion he showed him when his father died early on the tour. (Ironically, Underwood had been sharing with Pocock on the previous tour of India when his father had also died.) On his return from the funeral, he was told that Underwood had specifically asked to keep sharing with him and was a great help to him in their tactical discussions. Cope proved a highly capable reserve spinner and when injury forced Chris Old to miss the final Test, everybody said, 'Get yourself geared up, Geoff, it will be you.' 'Then Derek came in and put his arm around me,' recalled Cope. "I'm sorry, you should have played, but they're playing Mike Selvey." He was a good mate, Derek. When he sees me now, he says, "Hello Roomy.""

Boosted by their early form in the provincial games and convinced that the Indian batting was suspect to pace, England approached the first Test in good heart. On a slow Delhi pitch which nullified the threat from Bedi and Chandrasekhar, they scored 381 (Amiss 179) and brushed India aside for 122 with debutant paceman John Lever capturing seven wickets. Recalling the Englishmen's incessant appealing, Gavaskar turned to Knott and warned him that if the Indian fielders started appealing with the same frequency, they would stand no chance, a warning that Knott heeded.

Following on, India had to contend with Underwood, who toiled for 44 overs on a slow turner to take 4-78 including the prized one of Gavaskar caught at slip for 71. 'I did not think the great Sunil Gavaskar would be a threat,' recalled Greig. 'He had a real problem with Underwood. If he did not get out to him, then he would be dismissed by another bowler because Underwood had put him under pressure. He could not pick Underwood's straight ball.'

A throat infection threatened to keep Underwood out of the Calcutta Test but desperate to do his duty, he willingly succumbed to Greig's entreaties to play, as the captain recollected, 'Breakfast time brought good news. Derek Underwood declared himself fit enough to play. I knew in my heart that he was anything but 100 per cent, but a spot of cruel psychology had worked in my favour. Deadly, you see, missed the vital third Test on our previous Indian tour four years ago, because he lay out in the sun for far too long and subsequently suffered sunstroke. I had often teased him about it since, for the Test had been lost and I knew he blamed himself. These past few days I have constantly reminded him, imposed on his conscience – as it were. Call it unfair if you will, but he opted to play because he felt he had to and that was the object.'

As luck would have it England fielded first in the blistering heat and Underwood, feeling wretched down at long leg, vomited, convincing Greig that he had been brave even to play. At the end of the day in which he bowled 13 tidy overs and took the vital wicket of Viswanath with his slower one, he returned straight to bed.

On a turning pitch, a defiant century from Greig gave England a lead of 166 before Underwood stunned the large crowd by bowling Gavaskar with one that kept low. A brief flurry of boundaries from Brijesh Patel threatened to ruin his figures at which point Greig stepped in and, without consulting him, switched to a more defensive field. Brearley, recalling the scene, wrote, 'I still have a vivid mental image of Underwood burned red, sweating, his trousers dusty, sagging and stained, his feet splayed Chaplin-like, standing forlorn at the end of his run-up while Greig towering beside him, imperviously directed the men to far-flung outposts of the field.'

Despite their desperate plight at the close – 18 behind England with only three wickets left – 70,000 turned up the next day to witness the last rites. Underwood proved too good for Erapalli Prasanna and Bedi and England eased to victory by ten wickets.

The third Test at Madras was marred by the unsubstantiated allegations of ball-tampering by India's captain Bedi against seamer John Lever, whose five wickets in India's first innings had given his team the upper hand. He was helped by Underwood, whose 17 overs conceded a mere 16 runs and gained him two wickets. One of these was the promising Brijesh Patel, who was bowled by a beauty which pitched on leg and knocked back his off stump. 'That was a delivery which would have foxed most of the batsmen in the world, so quickly did it move after pitching and so big was the turn,' recalled Gavaskar.

At 69/4, India looked to their young tyro Dilip Vengsarkar to hold the fort. Martin-Jenkins wrote, 'The young batsman needed all his skill, and a slice of luck, to keep out a superb over from Underwood in which he received almost every variation in that great bowler's repertoire – the quicker ball, the arm ball, the one from wide of the crease, the flighted delivery inviting a drive and a caught and bowled, and finally an orthodox spinner away from the bat which bit more than any ball Underwood had yet bowled and which spun off the edge to give [Chris] Old at gully a low chance which he could not quite take.'

Set 283 to win, Gavaskar and Mohinder Amarnath started cautiously before Underwood joined the battle. On another worn pitch affording him considerable turn he had both openers caught at short leg and sent back the nightwatchman off the last ball of the day. The next morning, he quickly disposed of Viswanath, aided by a brilliant low slip catch by Brearley, as India crashed to 83 all out, their lowest score in a home Test. During the celebrations to mark their series win, the first overseas for five years, Greig singled out Underwood, man of the match for his 6-44 match analysis. 'The guy's an unbelievable bowler,' he said. 'He keeps knocking down the vital man.'

Having had the rub of the green so far with the umpiring, England's fortunes changed drastically at Bangalore when countless decisions went against them. India won the fourth Test comfortably and drew the fifth Test at Bombay, but Underwood continued to trouble all their batsmen, not least Gavaskar, whom he dismissed six times in the series. 'It was tough to face Underwood in any condition,' Gavaskar later recalled. 'He was so accurate and bowled on the stumps. Since he had this ability to bowl quick when he wanted, you had to be in a position very early to play the shots. He was the toughest bowler I faced along with Andy Roberts.'

The same couldn't always be said for Greig. 'Deadly would bowl maiden after maiden wheeling away, hating to concede a run,' recounted wicketkeeper Roger Tolchard, who played as a batsman in India. 'Then Greigy would come on and bowl long hops and full tosses, go for runs and get wickets. It used to drive Deadly mad.'

Underwood took 4-89 in the first innings of the final Test and when Karsan Ghavri turned him to Fletcher at leg slip in the second innings he leapt up and down like an excited schoolboy. Not only had he taken five wickets for the first time in the series – and the 100th time in his first-class career – he also took his tally to 29 in the series, surpassing Fred Titmus's record of 28 wickets in India in 1963/64 and equalling Fred Trueman's haul of 29, the best for England in any series between the two countries. According to cricket journalist Dicky Rutnagur in *Wisden*, England won without another specialist spinner because of the tremendous effectiveness of Underwood. 'No longer could it be said of Underwood that he was principally a bowler for English conditions and that he had to be taken abroad "like an umbrella in case it rained". He exploited the conditions even more than India's own celebrated spinners. Accurate as always, he bowled with immense craft and wit – slower than before and with great variation. That the Indians never mastered him is borne out by the fact that he claimed as many as nine wickets in the last Test.'

Following a pleasant interlude in Sri Lanka, MCC journeyed on to Australia for the Centenary Test. In an absorbing game played in front of large crowds and legendary names at the MCG the initiative fluctuated throughout. In ideal bowling conditions, Australia, batting first, struggled throughout their innings with only captain Greg Chappell surviving for long. Although making only 40, he ranked it as one of his best innings, given the quality of the bowling, not least from Underwood, whose figures of 3-16 off 94 deliveries spoke for themselves. 'You just had to wait and wait,' Chappell wrote. 'Unless he gave you room it was hard to score.'

Their paltry total of 138 looked rather better once they had routed England for 95. Thereafter, it needed the heroics of Randall's 174 to keep his side in the game before Dennis Lillee's five wickets gave victory to Australia by 45 runs, the same result as in the corresponding match 100 years earlier. As players past and present mixed afterwards to pay deference to cricket's glorious heritage, most were totally oblivious of the coming storm that was about to rock the game to its foundations.

Chapter 8

A Glorious Decade

BY 1967 the efforts of Les Ames and Colin Cowdrey over the previous decade to revive Kent cricket finally came to fruition with a team of all the talents of which the county could be proud. Although reluctant to hark back to his playing days and inflate his achievements, Ames's record as arguably the greatest wicketkeeper-batsman of all time – the only one to score 100 centuries – won him a distinct following from senior committeemen to junior professionals. One of his greatest admirers was all-rounder Alan Dixon. He recalled watching him bat in the nets several years after his retirement and smashing the great Doug Wright all around Canterbury. 'Les only had to walk into the room and people wanted to hear what he had to say,' commented fast bowler Alan Brown. 'Having been a player himself, Les knew enough about people to understand the personalities involved,' remarked Underwood. 'He was very open, very straight and at times quite hard.' 'Les was tough,' concurred David Clark. 'If an individual or the team had a bad day he would use the appropriate strong language.'

At the same time, underneath an austere exterior, he cared deeply about his charges, consoling and encouraging whenever appropriate. According to his biographer Alan Hill, 'A whisper of praise from Ames was worth more than a gush of gratuitous compliments from anyone else,' while in Underwood's estimation he was very shrewd and sensitive in his dealings with people. 'Only 11 of us could play for Kent. He was keenly aware that those left out had to maintain their morale and he kept on top of the situation.'

'Les and Colin were both gentlemen,' recalled Asif Iqbal, who joined Kent in 1968. 'They instilled discipline by the way they talked and treated people.' 'Colin Cowdrey and Les Ames had a big influence on all of us,' added John Shepherd, who, like Asif, was one of Kent's greatest stalwarts. 'Colin was a great encourager. You learned so much. He brought a family life to the team by organising golf days, club dinners and simple acts of kindness.' Alan Ealham described him in similar terms, calling him a father figure. 'He helped you with your cricket, but he helped you off the field as well in your private life. If there was someone who felt left out because he hadn't got a bonus he'd raise it with the committee. He was always looking after the players.'

Bob Woolmer, another of the younger players, recalled the excellent team spirit – people chatted to each other till late of night – and Cowdrey's benign influence be it his technical help, not least in the middle, the notes of encouragement or listening to their opinions. 'What Colin did was mould a team that wanted to win,' said Woolmer.

This tough and tender approach translated in the way Kent played their cricket, individual identity blending with the team ethic and entertaining the crowd with their will to win. At a time when National Service discipline and deference were still the norm, great players such as Cowdrey, Knott and

Underwood never lost their self-effacing humility. 'They were all good blokes, that's why we were so successful,' reflected Norman Graham. 'There were strong characters, but everyone respected each other. There were no egos in the side.' In particular, he recalled the camaraderie between the four quick bowlers, David Sayer, Alan Brown, John Dye and himself, even when one or two of them missed out. That team spirit was evident to Asif Iqbal. 'Everyone wanted their team-mates to succeed and that was the great thing about Kent. A happy side will do well.'

The players also forged a great rapport with their supporters. While their success and style of play undoubtedly strengthened that bond, much of it was down to their approachability. Taking their cue from the likes of Dixon, Brown and Brian Luckhurst, their roots deep in the Kent soil, they thought nothing of engaging with spectators, many of whom sat in the same place on the boundary day after day, strolling around the ground and signing autographs. On one occasion Underwood was about to drive out of Canterbury at the end of a tiring day when he came across a group of boys seeking his autograph. Turning off the engine, he lined them up in a row and spent some 15 minutes signing their books. Essex supporters in contrast weren't quite so fortunate. Approached by some autograph hunters in the car park at Brentwood, Underwood pointed to a nearby car, knowing it to be Knott's, and told them to wait there before departing quickly by another exit.

As with many young professionals entering the world of first-class cricket in the early 1960s, Underwood soon learned his place in the dressing room hierarchy. Naturally polite and self-effacing, he said little but was very open to advice from senior professionals and his former coach Claude Lewis, who watched every ball from the scorebox. 'Derek always listened and that is why he learned so quickly,' recollected Dixon. Quickly discerning his potential as a match-winning bowler, something that Kent had lacked over recent years, Cowdrey took a special interest in him and was never short of guidance and encouragement, not least on their many journeys together on the road. In his first season he organised a net for Underwood with Keith Miller, the former Australian all-rounder, and he bowled him with his quicker ball. Stuart Leary called it the 'Keith Ball' and for the next few weeks he was the butt of some irreverent humour. Leading the japes was vice-captain Peter Richardson, a renowned prankster, who ribbed him for his ill-fitting Hector Powe suits. It so happened that when Kent stayed in Nottingham there happened to be a Hector Powe shop across the road and Richardson told Underwood to meet him at nine o'clock the next morning. 'Like a fool I was pacing the hotel lobby at 9am and still pacing it half an hour later waiting for Richardson,' Underwood recollected. 'He, of course, was up in his room, chuckling to himself and enjoying his breakfast in bed.'

With cricketers spending much time on the road, there was plenty of opportunity for getting to know their fellow passengers. Having passed his driving test, Underwood bought a Rover with the engine in the back of which he was very proud and travelled principally with Shepherd, Alan Ealham and Asif. The former recalled him as 'a real Englishman'. 'You couldn't meet a nicer guy, such a gentle soul.' He was excellent company, singing along to Sandie Shaw, Petula Clark and Herman's Hermits. (He also liked classical music.) Living close to Asif, Underwood used to pick him up at his home at Orpington and deposit him back at the end of the day, spending the time discussing Pakistan culture when they weren't talking about cricket. On trips down the M2 to Canterbury and Dover, when they used to stop at a service station for breakfast, Underwood, a great lover of his food, tried to persuade Asif to try egg and beans or steak and chips, his favourite evening meal.

One lesson Underwood instilled in Asif occurred in his first year when he gave his wicket away in the 40s. On returning to the pavilion, Underwood said to him, 'Iqqy, what was that shot? You were playing so well!' When Asif replied that he played cricket for fun, which was the tradition in Pakistan, Underwood said, 'Playing here is not for fun, but to win for the team and the supporters.' It was the first time that Asif heard something about cricket as a livelihood and it really ingrained in him a professional ethic which he helped establish back in Pakistan, leading to better results and more secure careers.

As Kent looked forward to building on their 1966 position of fourth in the Championship, their best since 1947, their hopes were boosted by the arrival of Barbadian Shepherd, an extremely talented all-rounder who enthused the crowds with his spectacular hitting. Despite the atrocious weather in May, they gave early notice of their potential by dismissing Yorkshire for 40 at Bradford with Norman Graham bowling out Boycott for a pair.

In a season in which the Kent attack lay waste to many a county side, Underwood enjoyed a particularly productive July with 7-78 against Pakistan at Canterbury, 6-28 against Leicestershire at Folkestone, 7-35 and 5-15 against Hampshire at Maidstone and 7-38 and 7-44 against Sussex at Hastings. One of his victims in the second innings was Greig, playing his first season in the Championship. After Underwood's first two balls reared off a length, passing his nose, the 6ft 7in Greig let out an expletive and tended to the pitch; he tried to smash the next ball but only succeeded in mis-hitting to gully and departed for nought.

In front of a capacity Sunday crowd at Maidstone (Sunday play in the Championship was introduced for the first time that year) Hampshire were bowled out twice in one afternoon for 58 and 31, their last six wickets falling on the same score. Incensed by the capricious nature of the pitch, their captain Roy Marshall angrily denounced it, expressing a widely held view that Kent pitches were deliberately doctored for Underwood's benefit. Yet while the deteriorating standard of pitches at several of the Kent grounds was undeniable, it was part of an overall trend that afflicted the English game in the 1960s. It is also worth recording that 54 of Underwood's 111 Championship wickets that season were taken at home compared to 57 away and that according to *Test Match Special* scorer Bill Frindall, his wickets per match ratio in his first seven years was 3.78 in home games compared to 4.58 in away ones.

Kent's success proved a double-edged sword because the selection of Cowdrey, Knott and Underwood for the final two Tests against Pakistan compromised their chances of winning the Championship. They then suffered a further blow with the loss of Luckhurst with a broken finger sustained against Fred Trueman in the top-of-the-table clash with Yorkshire at Canterbury. The return of the 46-year-old Godfrey Evans as to Knott's replacement was an added attraction for the vast crowds that flocked to Canterbury Week, but to no avail as Kent lost to Yorkshire by seven wickets.

After draws against Essex and Derbyshire, Cowdrey's men returned to winning ways against Glamorgan at Gillingham. Once again, the dubious nature of the pitch drew the ire of defeated Glamorgan captain Tony Lewis after 26 wickets fell on the final day, Underwood being the difference between the sides with match figures of 11-73.

Two days later the teams met again at Cardiff and Kent, without their Test players, batted abysmally to lose by an innings. They finished in style by beating Warwickshire and Essex in Dover Week, the latter somewhat bleary-eyed after an evening night out on the ferry to Boulogne. Although Yorkshire, with a game in hand, were favourites to win the Championship (they duly accomplished this with an innings victory over Gloucestershire), Kent finished runners-up and achieved their best position since 1928. Leading his players out at the end of the Essex game to take a bow from the appreciative crowd, Cowdrey told them that his side were 'a crowd of good blokes, non-blasé, non-cynical who have thrown themselves into it every day'. As a young side they were going to get better, and he hoped that the next five years would be triumphant ones for Kent. Alluding to Underwood's accomplishments of the previous year, Cowdrey didn't expect him to repeat them. To head the national bowling averages yet again with 136 wickets at 12.39 was a phenomenal achievement, he added.

Pipped to the Championship by Yorkshire, Kent found consolation in the Gillette Cup, the popular 60-over competition introduced in 1963 and won in the first two years by Sussex. Yet to beat a first-class county in the competition, they rectified that record with a 42-run defeat of Essex in the second round before overwhelming Surrey at the Oval thanks to Alan Dixon's

7-15, his victims including Micky Stewart, John Edrich and Ken Barrington.

Drawn at home against Sussex in the semi-final, they turned in a princely performance in front of the largest crowd at Canterbury since the visit of Don Bradman's 1948 Australians. Batting first in glorious sunshine and on a perfect pitch they lost Denness early but a vibrant second-wicket partnership between Luckhurst and Shepherd paved the way for a memorable exhibition from Cowdrey. Entering at 138/2, he graced the occasion with his felicitous timing and his 78 from 59 balls helped Kent to a total of 293/5.

Sussex began poorly and were never in the hunt once they lost Greig. Lashing out at Underwood, he skied two consecutive balls before he was bowled on the third.

Victors over Sussex by 118 runs, Kent faced Somerset in the final at Lord's. In a heady atmosphere, full of hops and cider, they batted first and received the soundest of starts from Denness and Luckhurst before the innings fell away after lunch. All out for 193, their prospects were further diminished when Somerset took tea at 51/0, but the Kent attack sucked the lifeblood out of their batting with their accuracy to give them victory by 32 runs and an evening's celebration at The Talk of the Town nightclub in Leicester Square. Later they were invited to dinner at the Carlton Club by leader of the Opposition Ted Heath, who as a young man used to cycle to Canterbury from his home in Broadstairs to watch Kent play. Recalling their victory, Underwood reckoned that he'd been bowling well without any success before claiming three late victims. That day lingered long in the memory of the Kent players, not only for their success but also for the thrill of playing before a full house at Lord's and giving their supporters a memorable day out. The desire to repeat it helped motivate them to further triumphs in the years to come.

The year 1968 brought two significant changes to the County Championship. The first was the innovation permitting each county to engage overseas players without residential qualification; the second was the introduction of bonus points for runs scored and wickets taken in the first 85 overs of each first innings of a match. The registration amendment didn't stop Yorkshire, still dependent on home-grown players, from winning the Championship for the 31st time. Once again Kent finished runners-up, their failure to gain enough batting bonus points costing them dear.

Having won the lottery with their signing of Shepherd, their latest acquisition, Asif Iqbal, the Pakistan all-rounder, proved another shrewd investment. A natural entertainer who electrified the crowds with his scintillating strokeplay, he also inspired his team-mates with his positive outlook and, like Shepherd, was central to the club's success over the coming decade.

Galvanised by his ambition to win back his Test place, Underwood was the scourge of Derbyshire and Somerset in Gravesend Week in mid-May. During his 7-46 against the latter, he came up against their young Australian batsman Greg Chappell for the first time. Describing his 61 scored out of 134/9 declared, Chappell's biographer Adrian McGregor wrote, 'Greg's confrontation with Underwood was characteristic of their battles to come in situations when Greg was running out of partners. He hit nine fours and one six, punching Underwood off his back foot and driving with a free-swinging bat.'

Underwood continued to be a terror on damp and crumbling pitches, not least in successive matches against Glamorgan at Swansea and Hampshire at Gillingham. For the second year running, the Gillingham pitch was the subject of adverse comment as Underwood made Hampshire's final innings a nightmare. 'I shall never forget the game at Gillingham in 1968 when Hampshire were bowled out for 58,' recalled Kent cricket writer Dudley Moore. 'Derek clinched 7-17 and what the Hampshire players said about the pitch was nowhere near printable. Derek made the ball lift and turn in alarming fashion with catching almost as big a nightmare for close fielders as the unfortunate batsmen. The ball flew everywhere, and I have a lasting memory of Stuart Leary being congratulated after he clung on to one catch using his knees.' 'The wonder of it was how on earth we managed to score 17 runs off him,' recalled Barry Richards. 'One ball he bowled to Barry Reed ... Reed played forward and the ball hit him smack in the face.'

'You can appreciate it if Underwood adopts a just can't win attitude,' reported John Evans, sports editor of the *Kent Messenger*. 'There he stands, proudly top of the first-class averages yet again with 62 wickets at a cost of less than 11 apiece, and a lot of people seem to put it down to the fact that he operates on dodgy pitches. Whatever the rights and wrongs of the Gillingham pitch, he bowled magnificently, hitting the suspect patches with uncanny accuracy and making the ball whip across the batsman, so much so that at times the Kent players were applauding Knott's stops.'

As with the previous year, the season ended on a high note with victories over Northamptonshire and Glamorgan, their rivals for runners-up, at Folkestone with Underwood sharing the spoils with Graham, Dixon and Shepherd.

After the success of the two previous years, Kent greatly disappointed in 1969, dropping to tenth place in the Championship. They began well enough with Underwood helping them to convincing victories over Middlesex at Lord's and Essex at Brentwood, but injuries and Test calls then took their toll with Cowdrey and Shepherd, also on tour with West Indies, missing most of the season and Asif the last six games.

Hopes were much higher for 1970. At the club's centenary dinner at the Great Danes Hotel that spring, Ted Heath, preparing for a general election he wasn't expected to win, remarked that until now 1906 was probably the club's most important year because it witnessed a change in government and Kent winning the championship. 'Now 1970… well what could be more certain?'

While Heath's optimism politically proved fully justified, it seemed greatly misplaced on the cricketing front, since Kent's start couldn't have been more dismal with only two Championship wins by the end of June. Symptomatic of their malaise was their game against Warwickshire at Gravesend. On a challenging pitch, Underwood took 14 wickets (7-103 and 7-110) but ended up on the losing side. In the first innings Rohan Kanhai straight drove him for six first ball on the way to a brilliant century, and in the second innings Dennis Amiss scored an accomplished 91, which he rates as one of his finest innings. A good friend of Underwood's since their tour of Pakistan in 1966/67, he thought him a highly intelligent bowler who worked batsmen out. He countered by using his pad and playing late. Caught behind off a no-ball, he turned to the dejected wicketkeeper and said, 'Bad luck, Knotty, it's my day.'

June brought little uplift and Cowdrey received a telegram from Heath, by now Prime Minister, following his election victory. 'I've achieved my ambition,' he wrote, 'but I'm a bit worried about yours.' In early July Kent were rooted to the bottom of the table and following an abject defeat by Sussex in the Gillette Cup, Les Ames had seen enough. Worried by the club's ailing finances – the previous year they'd made a loss of £2,671 – he called the team together at the beginning of Maidstone Week and spelt out a few home truths about their negative cricket, especially their lack of batting bonus points. The floor was then open to the team and out of those deliberations a new sense of purpose was forged. With the emphasis on attack, they scored at 100 runs an hour the next day to secure six batting points against Derbyshire before seeing off Hampshire with ease. A fortunate draw against Yorkshire at Sheffield then gave way to a ten-wicket victory against Sussex at Hove, a game notable for Underwood's absence owing to a very rare injury.

At the end of a frustrating Canterbury Week which yielded two draws, Kent travelled to Weston-super-Mare in torrential rain to play Somerset. After arriving at 2.45am they found themselves labouring in the field a few hours later. It needed an inspired spell of bowling from all-rounder Bob Woolmer to restore their fortunes; then with Underwood luring them to their doom in the second innings with some flighted deliveries, they rode out easy winners.

Such was the new-found spirit in the team that they overcame the absence of Cowdrey, Knott and Luckhurst on Test duty and Shepherd to injury to beat Gloucestershire at

Cheltenham. Things looked ominous when their batting faltered in their first innings, and it needed the last-wicket pair of Underwood and Dye to scramble the few runs they needed to save the follow-on.

In Gloucestershire's second innings, Underwood took six wickets, to give him 11 in the game, but Kent's challenge of making 340 on a turning pitch against John Mortimore and David Allen, two of the country's leading spinners, looked a forlorn one. Undaunted, Denness with 97 and Asif with 107 attacked with gay abandon and despite a late collapse, Kent emerged victorious by one wicket.

Dark horses now for the Championship, their match against Surrey at Blackheath assumed a crucial significance. Making up for lost time after bad weather, Kent played wonderfully attacking cricket. Set 263 to win in three-and-a-half hours and encouraged to go for glory by some deft captaincy from Cowdrey, Surrey remained in the chase throughout until with 12 needed off eight balls, Pocock, their number 11, was brilliantly caught by Asif on the long-off boundary.

From Blackheath to Folkestone and two memorable games for the Kent faithful who flocked to this historic ground with stunning views of the North Downs. In the first against Nottinghamshire, the Championship seemed a mere illusion when Kent, replying to their opponents' 376/4 declared, slumped to 27/5 in their first innings, but a resolute 156 not out from Luckhurst and 57 from Ealham kept them in the game.

When challenged by Sobers to score 282 for victory in three hours, Kent needed no second invitation. Denness and Luckhurst gave them a wonderful start and a late flurry from Knott saw them home with eight balls to spare.

Underwood with his elder brother Keith, a stalwart ally throughout his career.

Underwood playing for his father's team, Farnborough.

The keen fisherman.

The close-knit Underwood family. From left: Keith, Evelyn (mother), Leslie (father) and Derek.

Underwood with the family Airedale, Rustler, who once stopped play in a county game at Southampton by rushing on to the pitch.

The beginning of a unique partnership for Kent and England, Alan Knott and Underwood.

Underwood has Australia's John Inverarity lbw to win the fifth Test against Australia with minutes to spare: The Oval 1968.

Underwood's greatness as a bowler was based on his classical action.

Underwood has Australia's Doug Walters adeptly caught at slip by Peter Parfitt during his match-winning spell in the fourth Test at Headingley in 1972.

Underwood celebrates Kent's Benson and Hedges Cup win against Worcestershire with team-mates Asif Iqbal, Mike Denness and John Shepherd: Lord's 1973.

Derek and Dawn Underwood with their respective parents on their wedding day: October 1973.

England fielders celebrate the dismissal of Sunil Gavaskar caught by Bob Woolmer at short leg off Underwood: Madras 1977.

With two games to go, Kent were 12 points behind Glamorgan, the reigning champions, with a game in hand, and six points ahead of Lancashire. Another 20-pointer was needed against Leicestershire. Having bowled them out cheaply on the opening day, Kent then batted with such panache that they collected eight batting bonus points in their 85 overs, with 21 runs coming off the last one.

Leicestershire began their second innings soundly but in the closing overs Underwood took two vital wickets and cleaned up the next morning to help his side to a record 23 points, one of four games post-Maidstone when they gained over 20 points.

With Glamorgan only able to draw against Lancashire, Kent travelled to the Oval for their final game against Surrey as clear favourites. A spirited bowling performance in ideal conditions restricted Surrey to 151/9 declared and a Cowdrey century gained them the necessary points. As the game meandered to a draw on the final afternoon, the players could rest easy in the knowledge that they were champions for the first time for 57 years and that no county had ever come from so far behind to win. During the dressing room celebrations afterwards they were joined by Ted Heath, whose pre-season predictions had come true. A few weeks later he organised a celebratory dinner at Downing Street where Cowdrey presented him with the ball with which his team had been playing on the day of his election victory.

Kent began the defence of their title the following year with an innings win against Yorkshire at Bradford, Underwood the chief destroyer with 7-28 in the first innings. Off-spinner Geoff Cope tried to attack him and ended up with a broken nose as the ball cannonaded into his face. 'It was a rain-affected pitch,' he recollected. 'Andrew Dalton played. He charged Underwood and was out by more than six yards. He came in and said, "I shouldn't be expected to play on wickets like that." Of all stupid things I attempted to lap Underwood and got a faceful. I think I'm the only person that Derek has maimed.'

He was equally destructive in the return game in Canterbury Week with five wickets in each innings, but despite his overall tally of 97 wickets he lacked the necessary support, and with pneumonia ruling Cowdrey out for the second half of the season Kent had to settle for fourth place in the Championship.

Their attack was more suited to the one-day game with its emphasis on economy. 'Of course it is impossible to win all the time, but we always felt that in limited-over cricket the opposition would have to have everything going their way to beat us,' recalled Knott. He attributed their pre-eminence largely to the quality of their all-rounders such as Woolmer, Shepherd, Asif and Julien and to the brilliance of their fielding, led by the magnificent Ealham; his fielding down by the lime tree at Canterbury remains one of the abiding memories of that era.

In the Gillette Cup they enjoyed an easy passage to the final. Facing them were Lancashire, the new kings of one-day cricket led by their charismatic overseas players, Clive Lloyd and Farokh Engineer. Batting first in glorious weather, Lancashire were kept in check by the Kent attack, none more so than the free-scoring Engineer by Underwood, who bowled just short of a length outside his off stump. Only in the last few overs did they score freely to take their total to 224/7.

In reply Kent began shakily and were totally indebted to a heroic 89 from Asif. He played beautifully and while he was there victory seemed very much in their grasp, but when he was out to a spectacular catch by Lancashire captain Jack Bond at cover the resistance quickly crumbled and they lost by 24 runs. According to Asif, who was devastated by his dismissal thinking he'd lost Kent the game, it was the lowest point of his career. 'What made it particularly disappointing is that I believe we were the better side. We just didn't perform well as a team.' And yet for all their disappointment, the team still enjoyed themselves at the Savoy that evening. 'Great sides can forget one result and look forward to battles to come next season,' wrote Denness.

The year 1972 marked the official transition of the captaincy from Cowdrey to Denness, although the latter had deputised during his illness the previous one. A fine attacking batsman, a brilliant fielder and a man of the highest integrity, Denness's single-minded approach and lack of flexibility didn't make him a natural leader. According to Underwood, he was 'too nice a man' to be ranked among the best of captains, but in the one-day game his calm authority proved central to Kent's success.

In a dry summer of firm pitches, Kent began poorly, failing to win in the Championship until early July. Thereafter, like 1970, the tide began to turn with two victories in Canterbury Week and further wins over Worcestershire, Hampshire and Yorkshire enabled them to finish a distant second to Warwickshire. In the final game Underwood showed his partiality for Bradford by taking 8-70, the best for any bowler that season, a game incidentally where his promotion to nightwatchman left Julien, a centurion for the West Indies against England the following year, batting at number 11.

Once again foiled by Lancashire in the Gillette Cup, this time in the semi-final, where, in another gripping contest, they lost by seven runs, Kent found consolation in the John Player

Sunday League (JPL), the 40-over competition introduced in 1969 and in which they'd been runners-up in 1970. Although Underwood disliked the negative field placings associated with limited-overs cricket, his supreme control made him a talisman in any side. Adjusting his line to middle and leg, bowling a touch flatter and to six men on the leg side, he proved as difficult to dominate as in the longer version of the game. In addition to his economy, he was also a prolific wicket-taker as his career record of 346 wickets in the JPL would indicate.

Beginning with four wins in their first five games, Kent seemed destined to beat Middlesex at Folkestone. Requiring 128 to win they reached 126/6 in the 37th over, only then to lose their last four wickets at the same score, much to the disgust of Les Ames, who tore up the winner's cheque which he'd already made out to Kent. Losing two of their next three matches – the game against Hampshire was abandoned – they appeared to have blown their chance, but they won their next five games, while the leaders Leicestershire lost their final game to Yorkshire. Consequently, Kent needed to beat Worcestershire at Canterbury on 10 September to clinch the title. In overcast conditions, 12,000 saw Worcestershire, the 1971 champions, seize the early initiative as Ron Headley and Alan Ormrod between them struck five sixes off Underwood, his eight overs costing 61. At the end of his spell, he threw the ball on to the pitch in frustration.

A total of 191 to win appeared a tall order but Luckhurst, Johnson and Nicholls gave them a wonderful start and with Asif steering the ship safely into port Kent won by five wickets with two overs to spare, much to the jubilation of the crowd who gathered in front of the pavilion to salute their heroes.

Looking forward to the new season with keen anticipation, Kent had the perfect start against Sussex, who were under new captain Tony Greig, at Hastings, a ground smelling of fish and seaweed. After batting first in the biting cold and scoring 282/5 declared, they then found the elements very much in their favour on the second day when, on a drying pitch, Graham (5-13) and Underwood (5-43) disposed of Sussex for 67. Amid their victims was the young Johnny Barclay, making his debut for Sussex. Receiving his first ball from Underwood he thrust out his bat and pad to try and smother the spin only to be struck painfully on the end of the right thumb, from where the ball ballooned up to Cowdrey at second slip.

Barclay spent a restless night agonising over a king pair as the rain lashed down in torrents. Confronted with a waterlogged playing surface the next day, the barefooted Kent team minus Underwood, who was told to preserve his energies, began mopping up with rollers, blankets, forks and brooms before the local fire brigade turned up. 'We were lucky that firemen, who are involved in an industrial dispute, regarded our plight as an emergency,' Denness wrote after the game.

Thanks to their efforts and the appearance of the sun play miraculously began at 4pm. Underwood was immediately let loose on the hapless Sussex batsmen and, making the ball turn and lift viciously, he was unplayable. Just 78 minutes later it was all over, Sussex dismissed for 54, Underwood finishing with figures of 8-9. A World XI wouldn't have done any better, remarked Greig. It was all Barclay could do to survive one ball before departing once again, caught Cowdrey bowled Underwood for nought. On his return to the pavilion he expected a grim silence only to be greeted by his exuberant team-mate John Spencer, who shook him warmly by the hand and said, 'A very honourable first pair. Caught Cowdrey bowled Underwood twice. What could be more distinguished than that?'

Underwood's exploits won him a crate of champagne from the *Sunday Telegraph*, but in an otherwise dry summer his return was a meagre 35 wickets in the Championship. Although Kent were unbeaten in this competition until mid-July, the limitations of their attack, exacerbated by their injudicious dismissal of John Dye at the end of 1971, led to a surfeit of draws thereafter and a final position of fourth.

Their depth in batting and agile fielding once again found fulfilment in the one-day game. Determined to win the 55-over Benson and Hedges Cup inaugurated the previous year, they coasted through the zonal round and following a narrow 11-run victory over Hampshire in the quarter-final they saw off Essex in the last four to play Worcestershire in the final.

In front of a capacity crowd at Lord's, half-centuries from Luckhurst and Asif provided the platform for Kent's total of 225/7; then despite captain Norman Gifford's tactics of promoting wicketkeeper Rodney Cass and himself, both left-handers, on the premise that Underwood didn't like bowling to them, Worcestershire couldn't break out of his stranglehold, leaving D'Oliveira, batting at number seven, with too much ground to make up.

Chuffed with their 39-run win, the players and their families celebrated quietly at the Sportsmen's Club because of a vital JPL game against Northamptonshire at Brackley the next day. After an early loss to Hampshire, Kent had embarked upon a winning run that had taken them to the top of the table. Displaying the utmost professionalism, they totally outplayed

Northamptonshire, scoring 257 and dismissing their opponents for 67, Underwood mopping up with 4-9. His performance was typical of a year in which he headed the national JPL bowling averages as Kent retained their title with two games in hand.

Once the season had finished the club embarked on a highly enjoyable two-week tour of Canada, during which thy won five and drew two of their seven games. Playing on a variety of different surfaces, the one grass pitch they encountered at Winnipeg proved dangerous. Denness lost several teeth when batting and Underwood was too much of a proposition for the locals as Winnipeg were brushed aside for 33.

Although Test calls and injuries were problematic for Kent throughout this period, 1974 proved particularly onerous. Denness, Knott and Underwood were absent for over half the games because of Test calls, Asif missed most of the season because of the Pakistan tour of England and Julien likewise because of a serious ankle injury. In this depleted state, Kent slumped to tenth in the Championship; in the JPL they won their first seven games, but they faded thereafter, with inclement weather forcing the abandonment of two games, and finished in third place.

In the Benson and Hedges Cup, they narrowly lost to eventual runners-up Leicestershire in a wonderful game of cricket, but they fared better in the Gillette Cup. Drawn once again against Leicestershire in the third round, they gained their revenge in front of the Canterbury faithful. A masterly century from Luckhurst gave them a perfect start and although Brian Davison meted out some rare punishment to Underwood, hitting him for 18 in one over, the latter disposed of the tail to help Kent to a 66-run victory.

Pitted against Somerset in the semi-final at Canterbury, Underwood described it as one of the most nerve-wracking games of his career. Before another vast crowd, Somerset batted first and struggled against an accurate home attack. On 95/4 at lunch their hopes rested on their new West Indian batsman Viv Richards. On a private tour of the Caribbean with Mendip Acorns the previous spring, Underwood had bowled to Richards in Antigua and had him clearly stumped, but the umpire, knowing that Richards was being assessed by Somerset for a possible contract, gave him not out. Now the boot was on the other foot because Richards, having hit Underwood for six, fell to him lbw and with the lower order contributing little, Somerset were all out for 154. Kent in turn lost early wickets, including Cowdrey clean bowled by an unknown paceman called Ian Botham, but Ealham and Woolmer kept their hopes alive, and Knott saw them home by three wickets.

Their reward was another tilt at Lancashire in the final, but in a miserable end to the summer rain washed out play on the Saturday and when the game took place on the Monday it was played under leaden skies and in front of a sparse crowd. On a seaming pitch Lancashire could only muster 118 but Kent found runs equally hard to come by and, once again, they were indebted to Knott for their four-wicket victory.

The momentum stalled the following year. In a sun-kissed summer Kent, outside contenders for both the Championship and the JPL, ended up winning nothing, leading to player unrest.

The 1976 season ushered in a new era following the retirement of Colin Cowdrey after 25 years with the club. The team soon lost the services of Luckhurst because of a broken knuckle and with their limited bowling resources they slipped to 14th in the Championship, their lowest position since 1957. The fact that the supremely fit Underwood had to limp off with leg and back trouble in the final game told of the toll that bowling in sustained heat had placed upon him. Although Kent's leading wicket-taker, he took only 48 in the Championship at an average of 27.47. His best return by far came early on with 7-56 against Worcestershire at Worcester, one of his victims being an aggrieved Basil D'Oliveira, who claimed he was given out caught off his thigh after a concerted appeal from Kent's close-in field. When Knott expressed his regrets about the dismissal to captain Gifford that evening, it still touched a raw nerve with both him and D'Oliveira.

Once again, the club found solace in the limited-overs game. A 30-run win over Nottinghamshire at Canterbury in the quarter-final led to a classic semi-final against Surrey at the Oval. A polished century from Denness gave Kent the early advantage as they made 280/3 in their 55 overs, but Surrey began strongly and remained in contention until Underwood took the last three wickets in five balls to give Kent victory by 16 runs.

In a repeat of the 1973 Benson and Hedges Cup final, Kent once again squared up to Worcestershire and in a similar match to the previous one they emerged triumphant by 43 runs. Requiring 237 to win, Worcestershire were always behind the asking rate. In a model mid-innings spell, Underwood, bowling a leg-stump line, gave nothing away and snared three top-order batsmen all caught by Johnson on the square-leg boundary as they hit out in desperation. Even a brilliant 50 from the injured D'Oliveira, batting at number seven with a runner, proved too little, too late.

Emulating their double triumph of 1973, Kent also won the JPL after losing three of their first five games. Thereafter they played to their potential and come their final game at Maidstone they stood an outside chance of winning. In the event they thrashed Gloucestershire while the favourites Somerset lost to Glamorgan by one run and, having tied on points with Essex, Kent won on a faster run rate.

Two trophies that year and six in five years, however, couldn't save Denness from losing the captaincy, an injustice that almost certainly would not have occurred had Les Ames still been manager. As with any leader there had been dissenters and certainly there were those such as Norman Graham and Bob Woolmer who thought him too remote and inflexible. More important, manager Colin Page was no admirer, while certain committee members hankered after the glamour of the Cowdrey era. During the previous year when Kent had failed to win anything for the first time in six years, there was enough discontent in the dressing room to trigger a team conference at Swansea, where opinions were freely aired. The committee, who were never interested in what Denness had to say, alluded to Kent's lowly position in the Championship in their 1976 report, but these were minor squalls in an otherwise settled climate. Kent won two trophies in 1976, lending weight to Knott's opinion that Denness was the best captain under whom he played.

Looking to the future, Denness indicated to Page in mid-July that he would be willing to stand down from the captaincy in favour of Johnson, a stipulation which wasn't his to make as he later acknowledged. His offer proved fatal because Page and his opponents on the committee saw it as an opportunity to remove him from office, although they expected him to fall on his sword, sparing them the burden of wielding the axe. After weeks of silence and obfuscation, Denness had it confirmed that he'd been dismissed and departed to Essex in high dudgeon.

Whatever the rights and wrongs of Denness's dethronement, the Kent committee made a wise choice by appointing Asif as his successor. His infectious enthusiasm proved a tonic to a side boosted by an influx of talented new players such as batsmen Chris Tavaré and Christopher Cowdrey, fast bowler Kevin Jarvis and wicketkeeper Paul Downton.

In addition to inconsistency in the JPL, Kent lost in the third round of the Gillette Cup, beaten by Middlesex by two wickets in a thrilling game at Canterbury when Underwood didn't bowl. Mike Selvey recalls the bemusement in their dressing room at his non-appearance – their spinners Norman Featherstone and Phil Edmonds had bowled 22 tidy overs between them – and assumed he was being kept for the denouement. As it was, the ninth-wicket pair needed six runs to win off Julien's final over and they won with a ball to spare.

While a feckless batting display accounted for their defeat by Gloucestershire in the Benson and Hedges Cup final, they found their mojo in the County Championship. In a frustratingly wet summer, they began well and although they lost to Northamptonshire at the end of June they continued their momentum by beating Leicestershire at Maidstone and then winning both games in Folkestone Week in July. On a rain-affected pitch against Yorkshire, Underwood took 7-43 and only Geoff Boycott stood in his way until he was last out for 61, undone by the most celebrated partnership in cricket. Prior to that there had been a minor difference of opinion between wicketkeeper and bowler regarding Kevin Sharp, Yorkshire's promising 18-year-old left-hander, who kept lunging forward at Underwood and getting hit in the stomach. After a while Sharp turned to Knott and said, 'I don't know how I am going to score a run.' Knott replied, 'Keep still, play him off the back foot and knock him to square leg,' advice which Sharp followed. Hearing this conversation, Underwood turned to Knott and said, 'What the hell do you think you're doing? You're coaching him,' to which Knott countered, 'He's only young, he needs to learn.'

They continued to win whenever the weather permitted it, but with so much playing time lost in August their lead began to wither. In the penultimate game against Sussex at Hove Underwood achieved his only hat-trick in first-class cricket when he sent back Imran Khan, John Snow and Arnold Long, stumped by Knott, but with rain putting a premature end to proceedings they ceded first place to Gloucestershire on the eve of their final game against Warwickshire. Middlesex too were in the running for honours, sharing the same number of points as Kent, and while Gloucestershire surprisingly lost at home to Hampshire, they beat Lancashire on the final afternoon to take 16 points, thereby throwing down the gauntlet to Kent.

In bowler-friendly conditions at Edgbaston, Asif's men, batting first, were all out for 118. Warwickshire also struggled in reply, and it needed a gritty 79 from Alvin Kallicharran to give them a lead of 63 on first innings.

In Kent's second innings, half-centuries from Woolmer, Shepherd and Ealham kept their hopes alive, before Warwickshire, needing 254 to win, collapsed to 27/5. A century from Geoff Humpage kept the champagne on ice until he was last out, giving Kent victory by 27 runs and a share in the Championship, the first shared one since 1950.

The furore over WSC led to Asif losing the captaincy to Ealham, a popular, respected professional who succeeded in maintaining a harmonious atmosphere in the dressing room. (See next chapter.) Although they were without Knott because of business commitments in his Herne Bay sports shop, they had the rare luxury of being able to play their internationals throughout the summer. While missing the chance to play for England, Underwood found it less stressful and enjoyed the opportunity of getting to know the younger players. In a year in which he bowled 815 overs, his supreme fitness once again proved invaluable. The year before he and Norman Graham had enjoyed a late night out, drinking seven or eight pints each and when the next morning physio Tony Toms put them through circuit training, he was amazed by his excellent physical shape.

The camaraderie of the dressing room helped him cope with the loss of his father Leslie, who having survived two heart attacks, collapsed and died of a third one at Charing Cross station on the May Bank Holiday. His death proved a shattering blow to all the family, but Evelyn was nothing if not indomitable and she continued to be a regular at Kent games, sitting next to her good friend Penny Cowdrey, willing her son on. Later, when Keith and his family moved to Biggin Hill in 1983 she would take her grandson Kevin, a budding cricketer at the Orpington club, to Canterbury. In 1988 Underwood asked her to accompany him to the launch of Dudley Moore's *The History of Kent County Cricket Club* but when E.W. Swanton discovered that she didn't have an official invitation he asked her to leave, much to her son's disgust.

Determined to prove the sceptics wrong about his continued commitment to Kent, Underwood's twin objectives for 1978 were winning the Championship and taking 100 wickets, both of which he accomplished in a summer of indifferent weather and rain-affected pitches. Aside from a comprehensive defeat by runners-up Essex at Ilford, Kent began in imperious form and never let up until the final two games, by which time the Championship had been all but settled. Rarely out of the action, Underwood combined with off-spinner Graham Johnson to inflict defeats on both Sussex and Surrey at Tunbridge Wells prior to their demolition of Surrey at the Oval, where conditions were very much in his favour. Having taken 4-13 in the first innings, he followed up with 9-32 in the second, the best return of the summer, as Surrey lost 18 wickets in just over four hours. Maidstone Week proved equally profitable, Underwood's 19 wickets seeing off Derbyshire and Glamorgan.

It said much for Paul Downton's promise behind the stumps that Knott wasn't badly missed. A law student at Exeter University, his arrival on the first-class scene as Knott's deputy the previous year was so spectacular that he was taken on England's tour of Pakistan and New Zealand as Bob Taylor's deputy. With Kent desperate to aid his development at a time of great uncertainty, Knott agreed to take a sabbatical, a gesture which Downton thought highly magnanimous. He described keeping to Underwood as a thrilling experience and a wicketkeeper's dream 'because he was so accurate, and you knew where the ball was going. He always bowled very straight. All you had to do was pick the arm ball.'

Downton also recalled Underwood's help and encouragement towards him. 'He could have been resentful without Knott, but he accepted the situation.'

Kent's march to the Championship was temporarily halted by another date at Lord's in the Benson and Hedges having beaten Nottinghamshire in the quarter-final at Canterbury and Somerset in the semi-final at Taunton. In a one-sided game, Derbyshire's decision to bat first rebounded on them as they lost three early wickets, including captain Eddie Barlow, the South Africa all-rounder, yorked by Underwood, who conceded a mere 22 runs from his 11 overs. Needing 148 for victory, they won comfortably owing to a solid 79 from Woolmer, giving them their third Benson and Hedges triumph in six years.

Back with the Championship, Underwood and Johnson combined to beat Leicestershire in the first game of Canterbury Week and Warwickshire were all set to suffer a similar fate following Underwood's 7-38 in their first innings, only for rain to rescue them.

The weather failed to save Gloucestershire from Underwood and a heavy defeat in the first game of Folkestone Week. When Kent faced Essex in the second game, they were 41 points ahead of their nearest rivals, but the latter had a game in hand. In front of large crowds, Kent eked out a useful lead of 42 on first innings and placed Essex on the defensive as Underwood, overcoming a sore back, bowled unchanged for three-and-a-half hours. *The Times'* Alan Gibson wrote, 'The damage had been done by Underwood on the not quite blameless Folkestone pitch. He is bowling very well at present. He took six wickets for 73, passing his 100 wickets for the season. This is a rare feat nowadays. Underwood is still a popular man in these parts, rightly, and all his supporters wish, as I do, that it were possible for him to go to Australia with England this winter. But he has chosen the mess of pottage.'

Left 185 to win in two-and-a-half hours, they lost early wickets and settled for a draw.

Although Kent were defeated in their final two games, they won the title by 19 points – Underwood finishing with 110 wickets at 14.49 – and went to Buckingham Palace in November when the Duke of Edinburgh, as patron and 12th man, presented the Lord's Taverners Trophy for the Championship. With their depth of talent, it seemed that Kent were destined for another decade at the top, but unknown to them the years of plenty were soon to be but a distant memory.

Chapter 9

Divided Loyalties

THROUGHOUT HIS career Underwood had kept to the straight and narrow, avoiding undue controversy, but all that changed with the introduction of Kerry Packer's World Series Cricket (WSC) in 1977. His decision to sign up to the riches on offer came at a price, especially when his commitment to England and Kent, his two greatest loves, was questioned. 'Derek would always conform,' commented Dawn, 'so for this to crop up was enormous.' Recalling the whole affair she wrote, 'It became an obsession in our house, often resulting in me wishing I'd never heard the dreaded name of Packer. Derek was worried and concerned and I found myself biting my lip and trying to give him encouragement and belief that he'd made the right decision.' She reckoned that had he not been married with a family, he wouldn't have joined.

Cricket had always been a poor man's game, not least during the inflation-ridden 1970s. Between 1973 and 1977, the cost of living rose by 96 per cent, whereas the remuneration for an England cap in that period had risen only by 40 per cent from £150 to £210. At the same time, the basic pay of capped county players averaged £2,600 a season, rising to perhaps £3,000 with bonuses, placing them below the average wage of a skilled worker.

In addition, professional cricketers weren't accorded the same rights as employees in any other job be it the lack of a proper pension scheme or the restrictions on moving to another county. Recalling the Kent committee as one of the stingiest on the circuit – although they did grant him two benefits – Underwood said, 'You would think twice about going out for a meal and try and save your meal allowance. Players had little or no representation on the committee and virtually no security of employment. There was a total lack of sensitivity and of understanding what the life of a professional cricketer was all about by those running the club in the 1970s.'

In Australia, relations between cricketers and their governing bodies were even more fraught. In an era of growing dissent, Test players were no longer content to play for the honour of representing their country, especially when money was flooding into the game through sponsorship. Their cause was taken up by media magnate Kerry Packer, the heir to an eminent dynasty renowned for its uncompromising approach to business. An inveterate gambler and sporting enthusiast, Packer saw in cricket a lucrative product unexploited by the authorities and twice bid for the exclusive right to televise the cricket in Australia, in 1975/76 and the following year.

Pre-emptively rejected out of hand by the Australian Cricket Board (ACB), Packer wasn't prepared to take his rebuff lying down. Discerning the defences of the cricketing establishment to be fraying, he went for the jugular. The issue on which he took his stand was players' salaries, which, despite some recent improvements, remained a pittance compared with other sports such as football, tennis and golf. Offering substantially better terms, he contracted 35 of the world's top cricketers for his WSC.

One of his leading agents in the recruitment of players was England captain Tony Greig, who fretted about the meagre return he was making from the game, as he explained in a letter to Packer. 'I am 31 and probably two or three Test failures from being dropped by England. Ian Botham is going to be a great player and there won't be room in the side for both of us. I don't want to finish up in a mundane job when they drop me. If you guarantee me a job for life working for your organisation, I will sign.' It was a request to which Packer was only too happy to accede.

Appearing with the MCC tour party to India on Thames Television's *This is Your Life* soon after their return on 30 March, Greig telephoned Underwood later that evening, saying 'he had a problem'. He rang again early the next morning, getting Underwood out of bed, to inform him about a new venture in Australia, a series of 'Tests' between an Australian XI and a Rest of the World XI. A natural salesman, Greig told him about the handsome pay cheque he would receive, but warned him that if he chose to participate, he would be unavailable to tour with England for the next three winters. While attracted by the significant sums involved of some £40,000 Underwood fretted about a possible Test and county ban, given the inevitable backlash that WSC would provoke.

The later question was addressed by Austin Robertson, a former Australian Rules footballer and trusted Packer lieutenant, at a meeting of potential WSC recruits at London's Churchill Hotel on 11 April. Robertson showed them copies of the standard form of contract and they discussed it among themselves. Their major concern was the effect WSC would have on the international game and the adverse reaction of cricket's governing body to it.

Later that day they went to the Dorchester to meet Kerry Packer. He explained that if this new venture was to be successful, the contracts needed to be rigorous and drawn up quickly. At the same time, he reassured them that he would do everything in his power to help them; both sides had to sign the contracts in a spirit of mutual trust.

Having met Packer, they returned to the Churchill Hotel where Underwood rather reluctantly signed up, since he'd wanted independent legal advice to clarify a few points, but to Robertson, time was of the essence. Aside from the proposals getting mired in delay should players seek legal advice before signing, he feared that news would leak out about the venture days before the Australian touring side left home for England, which could well scupper it.

Once Underwood had signed the contract, he took it to his solicitors, and they made various suggestions as to how it might be improved. Under the contract as it was originally drafted, JP Sports, Packer's new business interest, could theoretically stop him playing any cricket during the English summer. Later, when he met Packer's legal adviser, Underwood put the suggestions to him and it was partly because of him that the contracts were later amended, Packer giving a written undertaking that WSC players could play county cricket.

Despite being one of the country's leading cricketers, Underwood found it extremely difficult to achieve any degree of security. In line with other counties, Kent paid poorly. Even on the highest of scales used by the county in assessing the remuneration of its players, Underwood's basic salary was a mere £2,665 in 1975, £2,821 in 1976 and £3,155 in 1977. Other sources of income included £600 from winning bonuses, Test match fees of £210 per match and £3,550 from the tour to India in 1976/77, netting him about £7,600 in that tax year. Despite living at home until his marriage in 1973, he reckoned he would have found it very difficult to support his wife had he not had a benefit in 1975.

As he was away from home so often during the year, Underwood thought it essential that Dawn should join him on tour, but he never received any financial assistance in the payment of her flight either to Australia in 1974/75 or Sri Lanka in 1976/77. She stayed in Australia for six weeks but because wives were only able to spend 21 nights in the same hotel as the players, a ruling they deemed absurd, he had to find alternative accommodation for her.

What also concerned him was his lack of qualifications outside of cricket and his inability to forge an alternative career, epitomised by the casual winter employment he'd undertaken over the years. Consequently, he regarded WSC as a means of providing him and his family – their elder daughter Heather was born in February 1976 and Dawn was expecting again – with the security he had not been able to achieve throughout his career hitherto. He wrote, 'Under my contract with JP Sports, however, I am assured of being paid substantial sums to take part in world-class cricket of a very high standard during the three coming seasons and it is a great improvement to have one's future employment ensured in that way. Hitherto, I have never been asked whether or not I was available to play for a touring team, it being general practice that I should be kept waiting until the very last minute before a place in the team was offered to me.

'This insecurity about one's future is always at the back of a player's mind when he is playing, as is the possibility of being injured and having to withdraw from the game. (This can have frightful financial effects since the only insurance scheme which the Professional Cricketers' Association runs is poor.) As one draws towards the end of one's career (and as a slow bowler I think I might be able to play for a further five to ten years) this uncertainty looms larger in one's mind. As a result, I had been thinking for some time before the Super Tests proposals appeared that if a suitable business opportunity arose outside the game I would have to consider whether or not I should take it.'

Financial considerations aside, he was attracted by the idea of playing top-class cricket against the world's best players and overhauling the way the game was run. He didn't think a challenge to the game's governing body to be a bad thing, since these people, whatever their interest in cricket, weren't involved in it professionally in the sense that their jobs depended on their performance. 'In general, it seems to fear change (as advanced by their initial opposition to one-day cricket which has since proved extremely popular) and they incline to the view that "the game is the thing" and that it does not really matter who wins. It is not surprising therefore that insufficient attention is paid to the interests of the players and for this reason I would like to see a more professional approach to the game.' Aside from the inadequate salaries, he cited the length of tours, the surfeit of cricket played in the domestic season and the amount of time separated from players' families as problems that needed addressing.

When the news broke on 9 May that Greig, Knott and Underwood were joining WSC the reaction in England was overwhelmingly hostile. John Woodcock wrote, 'It is an astonishing situation when the captain of England goes to two of his best players (Knott and Underwood) and on behalf of an Australian impresario buys their services, knowing that it will almost certainly drastically reduce, if not bring to an end, their appearances for England.' In the *Sunday Express* Denis Compton accused the Packer players of betraying their country and the *Daily Mail*'s Alex Bannister wrote in a similar vein. 'The hardest things to say about the defection of Greig, Knott and Underwood ... is that they are selling out the game that has made them what they are.'

While accepting that they'd given much to the game, he alluded to Greig's extensive commercial contracts and Knott and Underwood's recently received income-tax-free benefits as amounts few citizens in less privileged walks of life could ever accumulate in a lifetime of hard saving. 'Nobody would say that Knott, Greig and Underwood were short of a bob or two.'

Further criticism came from Boycott, who accused the three players of 'prostituting themselves for money' and Mike Turner, the influential secretary of Leicestershire, who said that 'Greig's belief that these pirate international matches will benefit the ordinary player is nonsensical'. As far as the author and lyricist Tim Rice was concerned, if Greig was prepared to hawk his talents in any marketplace, would he like a role in *Jesus Christ Superstar*?

The Cricket Council, cricket's governing body in the UK, viewed Greig's clandestine role in the recruitment of players as a breach of trust in his relationship with them and, consequently, sacked him as captain. While Greig remained the main target of opprobrium, Knott was surprised by the level of hostility he encountered. He thought that most people would agree with his opinion that it was very healthy to have two employers in the

DEADLY

game. To those that knew him well, his decision to join Packer came as little surprise. Strongly of the view that wives should be allowed on tour – he'd nearly pulled out of the recent trip of India – he believed in the concept of WSC, since it strongly promoted player welfare.

In the case of Underwood, his defection occasioned more debate. His father Leslie said little but deep down he harboured reservations that his son had turned his back on English cricket and what it meant to him; chairman of selectors Alec Bedser thought it 'seemed out of character for a devoted team man'; and Bob Taylor, a leading opponent of WSC, expressed surprise that he'd signed. He later wrote, 'Underwood, a great bowler, would be an automatic choice for England for years to come and he always seemed a true traditionalist, a supporter of old-fashioned standards. I am sure he regretted the move, but he would never admit it.' Bob Willis, another opponent of WSC, was also baffled by his decision, since he regarded him as the soul of Englishness, reflected in his refusal to demand a pay rise in Australia in 1970/71 when an additional Test was arranged on the premise that to play for one's country was a huge privilege.

Wally Grout, the Australian former wicketkeeper, used to remark that when that great battler Ken Barrington walked out to bat in a Test match you could almost see the Union Jack fluttering behind him and the same could be said of Underwood. A true patriot in every sense, representing his country meant everything to him and he would go the extra mile to snatch victory or avoid defeat. And yet for all his professional approach to winning, he held dear many of the game's timeless values. In an era when sledging and gamesmanship had become more commonplace, he remained a model of deportment, clean shaven, smartly dressed and courteous to all, embracing the decorous traditions of Canterbury Cricket Week rather than the brash, gladiatorial version of the game envisaged by Packer.

According to the *Sunday Telegraph*'s Alan Lee, 'It wasn't that he [Underwood] was necessarily any better or worse than the other 40 odd names on the list. It was simply that, in the eyes of many, he had become an English institution.'

Unprepared for the sustained onslaught in the media, Underwood later defended his motives in an interview with Lee. 'There seemed to be a sense of horror that I, of all people, should have gone. People apparently put a lot of faith in records and thought I, too, should do so. But records don't bring up a family. I had been in and out of the Test side for years; there was no security. If I injured myself, I might never play again. They didn't think of that.' Later he told the High Court, 'One of my greatest worries has always been what would I do when my playing career is over? I have no qualifications. Up until now I have been unable to save much from my income. It's nice to feel that at last I am earning the sort of money that other international sportsmen have enjoyed for years.'

Once the news broke, Underwood, after consulting with Knott, contacted Kent chairman Walter Brice to ask if the two of them and Asif, another Packer recruit, could see him to explain their position. Brice readily agreed and they met on Friday, 13 May at Lord's, where Kent were trying to play Middlesex in the rain. At this meeting they explained their reasons for signing, reasons which from a purely financial point of view could be readily appreciated and assured him of their continued loyalty to Kent. Brice said that provided their participation didn't interfere with their club commitments he could not object to their signing. Later he reported to the Kent cricket sub-committee on 9 August: 'I think they were aware even at this stage that the steps they were taking might prejudice their future Test careers, but all were unanimous that the last thing they wanted was for their actions to interfere with their Kent careers and at that stage it was difficult to visualise how it could.'

All three players told Brice that they thought their actions were in their own interest and in the interest of professional cricketers in general, a view he found hard to accept. 'We parted on the understanding that Kent were now in the picture as to their intentions and that so long as the welfare of Kent County Cricket Club was not in any way impaired, we accepted the situation.'

Knott and Underwood also met Doug Insole and Donald Carr of the Test and County Cricket Board (TCCB), who were keen to discover more about WSC. After they confirmed that they wouldn't be available for overseas tours, Underwood had the impression that apart from this Insole and Carr were at a loss to know what to ask.

Knott and Underwood then talked to Mike Brearley. Both stressed that Packer was offering them a security they could never get from Kent or England. Both hoped that a compromise could be reached, but if not, they were prepared to face the consequences. Brearley told Underwood that he thought he had made a mistake if he had done anything to jeopardise his county career, 'which after all had been the fulcrum of his life since he was 17'.

With Greig axed as England captain, Brearley, his vice-captain in India, took over for the home series against Australia. On the advice of the TCCB, the selectors picked the team on merit, which allowed for the inclusion of Greig, Knott and Underwood, all of whom Brearley liked and respected. More important, he rated Greig's ability to get the best out of his men by involving them in team policy, a practice he continued. His reward was a loyal and united team in contrast to the faction-ridden Australians, 13 of whom had signed for Packer including captain Greg Chappell and vice-captain Rodney Marsh.

After an evenly fought draw at Lord's, England won the second Test at Old Trafford by nine wickets, helped by Underwood's 6-66 in the second innings. On the fourth morning with England leading by 139 with one wicket left, Brearley wanted Underwood to experiment by bowling over the wicket and into the rough just outside the right-hander's leg stump in Australia's second innings but knowing Underwood might be reluctant to depart from the norm, he asked Knott how he might react. Knott said, 'Deadly doesn't like his fields tampered with,' convincing Brearley that he should start talking to Underwood to sell his tactical ruse. He wrote, 'I reminded him that he could always revert to bowling round the wicket. I wanted to excite him about the thought of bowling over the wicket to Greg Chappell, who I thought would not enjoy the idea. As we talked Derek became more enthusiastic.'

By the end of the day Underwood had taken three wickets bowling over the wicket to right-handers including Chappell for an exquisite 112. Chappell wrote, 'He only bowled one bad ball all day, wide and short and it hit a crack and didn't bounce. I'd gone to give it the big one and when it stayed down it hit the bottom inside edge and back on to the stumps.' According to Christopher Martin-Jenkins, 'Underwood had rarely bowled better than he did after lunch, drawing on his vast experience of dry, easy-paced wickets, and varying his pace and trajectory with the skill of one of the greatest of all slow bowlers. Several overseas tours had made him adapt to different types of pitch, and although he still loathed anyone scoring off him he was more prepared to vary his flight and better able to operate over the wicket if conditions demanded it.'

Before setting out for Manchester for the Test, Underwood was contacted by Jack Bannister, secretary of the Professional Cricketers' Association (PCA), regarding WSC. He suggested that they meet in Manchester, but Underwood's late arrival put paid to that. Consequently, Bannister telephoned him again the following day just at a time when several reports were circulating that Underwood was about to renege on his contract, something he publicly denied. Bannister told him he would do anything to help and that the PCA would pay all his legal costs if he wished to break his contract with JP Sports. He also claimed that Packer was preparing to tear up all his contracts with the players in return for the exclusive television rights in Australia and that if he did break his contract he would be able to keep all the money he'd so far received.

Underwood listened to what Bannister had to say but suspecting that he might be acting on behalf of MCC and unimpressed with the PCA's failure to get its members a significantly better deal, he made it clear he intended to stay with Packer.

England welcomed back Boycott for the third Test at Trent Bridge after a three-year exile and gave a first cap to Botham. Both excelled in their seven-wicket win and their innings victory in the fourth Test at Headingley, which enabled them to regain the Ashes.

With the series now decided, the selectors were thinking of omitting the Packer players at the Oval. Their intentions were opposed by Brearley, who adopted a conciliatory line towards WSC throughout. 'Brearley made it quite clear to the players that he was only captain because of the advent of WSC and he stressed that it was Greig who had built up such a good side,' wrote Knott. 'Throughout the series with Australia in the summer of 1977 the atmosphere was perfect in the England dressing room, and the credit for that goes to Brearley and Greig.'

Brearley also understood the motives of the Packer players for greater financial security more readily than most, in line with his previous efforts to secure better terms for all players. During the Headingley Test he rejected a suggestion that a £9,000 cheque donated by several businessmen to the England team should exclude Greig, Knott and Underwood. He emphasised that they were a team and that every member should receive a share, which is precisely what happened.

England duly kept the Packer players for the Oval, a game ruined by bad weather. At the end of it, Underwood bade farewell to John Lever, who was touring Pakistan with England, and asked him to give his regards to Hyderabad's notorious Sainjees Hotel. Later that winter Lever and Willis sent him a postcard from there, greetings that meant much to Underwood. 'The fact that they'd taken the trouble to drop a line to Deadly their old mate made me realise that there was no direct animosity against me,' he later recalled. Rather their animosity was directed against what WSC stood for.

It was during the Oval Test that Bob Woolmer signed up for Packer. Originally strongly opposed to the enterprise, believing that his team-mates were placing their own interests above the general good of the game, he was won over by Knott and Underwood on a coach trip to Swansea in mid-July. They argued that Packer would improve the income of county cricketers, citing the recent Cornhill Insurance sponsorship that had raised England salaries from £210 a game to £1,000, and security of contracts, something very few cricketers then enjoyed.

Following an inconclusive meeting with the ICC at Lord's on 23 June, in particular their refusal to grant him exclusive Australian television rights, Packer told the waiting press that he would take no steps at all to help anybody. 'From now on it is every man for himself and let the devil take the hindmost.' Hostilities were further exacerbated by the ICC ban from Test cricket of all the WSC players from 1 October 1977, a ban which led to Packer contesting it in court to prevent third parties from inducing players to break their contracts.

Opposition to Packer also came from the TCCB, who announced on 10 August that WSC players would be banned from playing county cricket, a decision Underwood called 'disgraceful', and the PCA at their Extraordinary General Meeting at Edgbaston in early September. They voted in favour of the TCCB ban, many fearing that the county game would be devalued by players no longer fully committed to it. The idea that his fellow professionals wanted him outlawed left Underwood feeling slightly bitter and bewildered. If they succeeded, he confided to Alan Lee, the rift in the game would only widen and standards would decline.

He expressed similar sentiments to Graham Johnson, who was Kent's PCA representative. Of the belief that Johnson had told the Kent committee that the Packer players shouldn't represent the county again, he challenged him about his views, only for Johnson to explain that what he said wasn't necessarily what he thought; he was simply conveying a view within the club that Underwood and co couldn't serve two masters.

Against this backdrop, the Kent cricket sub-committee met on 9 August. Although the majority were unconcerned about what their Packer players did in the winter – one member, a former player and successful businessman, told Underwood he couldn't turn the offer down and put him in touch with his present solicitors for legal advice on the terms of his contract – David Clark thought otherwise. A former captain and chairman of Kent and the club's representative on the TCCB, he felt strongly about WSC and advocated a ban, a view supported by other club stalwarts such as Colin Cowdrey and E.W. Swanton, all of which influenced chairman Brice's position.

He remarked that the time was obviously approaching when the counties were going to be called on to make up their mind about their attitude to the TCCB. He reminded his colleagues that Kent received 30–50 per cent of its revenue from TCCB funds, either Test match receipts or sponsorship. The £26,000 they received from them in 1975 had resulted in an annual loss of £3,150 while the £47,000 obtained in 1976 had netted them a profit of £5,000. If county cricket as they knew it was to be preserved every effort must be made to support the TCCB. Brice said, 'This will call for some agonising decisions if in its attempts to save our cricket way of life the players who have contracted with Packer are banned from county cricket. To deny ourselves the services of the players concerned after their loyal and brilliant service to the county is indeed a terrible step to take, always provided it is legally enforceable which will be decided at the impending High Court case.'

This view was conveyed to the Packer players at a meeting called by Kent president Edward Wharton-Tigar on 20 August. They were told that the club wanted them to continue playing for them, but in the circumstances there was nothing they could do to prevent the proposed ban.

Packer's challenge to the TCCB began in the High Court on 27 September and lasted for seven weeks. Following Knott into the witness box, Underwood said that the biggest worry of his life was what career he would pursue once he'd finished playing since he had no qualifications. He also said that the PCA had tried to persuade him to break his Packer contract. On 25 November Mr Justice Slade ruled that to ban cricketers from Test or county cricket would be an unreasonable restraint of trade and an inducement to them to break their Packer contracts. A professional cricketer needed to make his living as much as any other professional man. Costs estimated at £250,000 were awarded to Packer's side. With success deemed highly unlikely for the cricket establishment, Underwood thought that the whole case was a flagrant waste of money.

Days before the Slade verdict he arrived in Australia without Dawn, who was about to give birth to their second daughter Fiona. With the South Africa and Pakistan players, who comprised the nucleus of the World XI, keeping to themselves and Greig and Knott living with their families in private accommodation, Underwood felt rather detached. Conscious that various players were missing loved ones, Packer went out of his way to look after them, not least at Christmas. After entertainment at the Chateau Hotel in Sydney, Underwood was thrown into the swimming pool fully clothed. In various conversations that he had with the journalist and broadcaster Henry Blofeld throughout the

Australian season he told him that he was having a wonderful time, but Blofeld remained unconvinced. Knowing him to be a great patriot, he always thought that he carried an element of guilt by resiling from what he stood for. 'If Underwood had realised at the time of signing what the reaction of the authorities would be I do not think he would have signed,' he wrote in his book *The Packer Affair*. 'Once he had done so he became a militant supporter of Packer – often a way of covering up doubts.'

Although the Packer players were depressed by the small crowds and lack of atmosphere – the Australian public preferred to watch a gripping Test series against India which Australia won 3-2 – WSC lacked nothing in intensity as the world cricketing elite competed against each other for substantial sums of prize money. 'It was brutal cricket out there,' recalled Barry Richards. 'Packer would not have it any other way.' When a rising delivery from Thomson hit Underwood on the hand, one of the fielders approached Underwood, asking, 'How's the hand?' 'It's the right hand,' said Underwood, to which the fielder replied, 'Shame, we were aiming for the left.'

Nothing better encapsulated the gladiatorial combat of the contest than the profusion of bouncers directed at all and sundry. Fourteen batsmen were hit that first year, and helmets became the norm for everyone bar Viv Richards and one or two others. The most startling innovation was the introduction of night cricket with black sightscreens, white balls and coloured clothing, which has proved WSC's most enduring legacy to the game.

The late finishes meant the players adapting to a new routine. Finishing at 10.30pm and returning to the hotel about midnight, Underwood liked to unwind with a couple of beers at the bar before going to bed at 1am and rising about 10am. The extensive hours and the quality of the opposition called for a greater emphasis on fitness and practice. According to World XI team-mate Mike Procter, Underwood was an old-style player who had to change his ways. He wrote, 'I'll never forget the look of horror on his face in the first year of WSC when he was told to run round the ground. He'd never had an injury in nearly 20 years of cricket, and he relied on simply bowling to keep himself fit. But he had to do it because you can't make an exception for him.'

The three WSC sides, Australia, West Indies and the Rest of the World, were to take part in three competitions: two series of Super Tests of three games each, the International Cup featuring 50-over games, and the International Country Cup based in the regional centres. In the first game, a practice one, between the WSC Australian XI and the World XI at Melbourne's VFL Park, watched by a crowd of 1,000, Greig introduced Underwood to the attack before lunch on the first day and minutes later he bowled Greg Chappell, playing no stroke. Blofeld wrote, 'I never imagined I could as an Englishman have watched that moment with such supreme indifference.' Beginning with 4-60, Underwood went one better against an Australian XI at Rockhampton, his 6-34 including a hat-trick. He continued to perform creditably and in the final of the Country Cup at Canberra his last-wicket stand of 57 with John Snow helped the World XI to an 85-run victory over the Australians.

No county was more riven by division than Kent where a sizeable section of the membership thought the four Packer players should face stern retribution for jeopardising the future of Test and county cricket. After much legal advice, the cricket sub-committee unanimously resolved on 12 January 1978 that, 'In view of the Court judgement and after careful consideration the Cricket Sub-Committee feel we have no option but to pay and consider for team selection the Packer players along with other members of staff.'

Their view was endorsed by the general committee at their meeting on 7 February. Accepting that they had implied contracts with the Packer players for the 1978 season and to sack them immediately would mean litigation for unfair dismissal, they voted by 14 votes to 7 to honour the implied contracts for 1978 which covered the summer only, implying that the players were free agents in the winter. At the same time, they acknowledged the divisions within the county caused by WSC and that their decision wouldn't please everyone.

When the general committee met again on 28 March, they discussed litigation costs if the players were sacked and who would be liable, the club or the committee. They then resolved by 15 votes to 11 that all players would have two-year contracts apart from the Packer ones who would have only a one-year contract and that 'Kent County Cricket Club will not require their services after Saturday 9 September 1978 and that they will be given formal notice in due course'.

According to Walter Brice, Kent's younger players were the envy of many other counties and unless places could be found for them it was only natural that they would begin to look elsewhere to the most serious detriment of the county. (An opposing view emanated from manager Colin Page, who thought the youngsters needed the guidance of the Packer players.)

The committee also replaced Asif as captain with Alan Ealham and stated that their promising young wicketkeeper

Paul Downton would play instead of Knott. 'And, to add insult to injury,' recalled Underwood, 'we were told that if we wanted to leave immediately, no one would stand in our way. We were all in shock. Poor little Knotty was practically in tears.' What particularly upset Underwood was the charge of disloyalty to the county he'd served with dedication for 15 seasons. He wrote, 'To say their action was hurtful was the understatement of the year. What we could not fathom was why we should be dismissed from Kent simply because we wanted to play cricket under another banner in another part of the world during the winter.

'There were people who seemed to think I would contaminate the place, that I would want an extra tenner a week, or that I would turn up in a better car than the committee man. All of which came down to jealousy. There were others who had genuine fears for the spirit of the team, but these were proved quite unfounded. I had no real problems with any of the players, although the younger ones couldn't understand how I could possibly give up any chance of playing for England. I pointed out that if they had been playing Test cricket for 12 years they would know it isn't all a bed of roses – I've lost count of the amount of times on a Sunday afternoon people have told me I've been left out of the England side.'

Their treatment outraged Les Ames, who thought of Underwood, Knott, Woolmer and Asif to be his proteges. Although now retired, he spoke out at Kent's Annual General Meeting (AGM) in April, calling their sackings 'a repugnant and distasteful decision'. 'I had a close association with all four players and have always considered them model examples of how professional cricketers should behave. Two of them are among the greatest cricketers to have played for Kent. I am very anti-Packer, but another way must be found to solve the problem.'

His show of loyalty saw him heckled by sections of the membership, an astonishing rebuke to one of Kent's greatest servants. 'Les was very brave,' recalled Underwood. 'He was being loyal to the players who'd done so well for Kent over the years. He knew that we cared and saw very little justification for our sackings.'

According to Underwood, Ames, as a former player, recognised the overriding claim of security at the heart of the contentious issue. 'Kent were not offering us contracts and this man from Australia was. Les was 100 per cent behind us in a worrying and traumatic time.'

Ames's attempt to rescind the sackings was heavily defeated at the AGM. According to Kent secretary Maurice Fenner, the vote was so overwhelming that it was right to assume the action of the committee fully reflected the views of the membership. The committee's hard line was strongly supported by cricket writer Roger Fowle in the *Maidstone Telegraph*. 'Kent's brave decision to take a stand on the Kerry Packer issue is to be applauded. The county will inevitably suffer a reaction for two or three years after the departure of Knott, Underwood and Woolmer, but the decision must be in the club's long-term interests. Kent, unlike some counties, are fortunate in having a wealth of young talent and to have retained the Packer men would have stifled their development.'

In fact, the sackings created widespread unrest among more moderate members. Their case was taken up by Dennis Fowle, a lifelong member, and Terry Goodrich, who argued that they had been treated too harshly. The committee were primarily responsible to Kent and their two prime duties were to work for playing success and financial security. Considering their decision to be detrimental to Kent cricket, they wrote to the *Sevenoaks Chronicle* and *Kentish Advertiser* inviting members to sign a petition calling for the reinstatement of the players.

Despite securing many more than the 100 signatures needed to call an extraordinary meeting, Fowle and Goodrich held their fire, hoping to avoid undue division and acrimony. They did, however, present the petition to new chairman John Pocock, urging a change of heart and threatening to call that meeting if the committee refused to give ground.

The Packer players also had the support of their team-mates who sympathised with their fight for financial security and captain Ealham lobbied the committee to reverse its decision. The fact that Underwood, Asif and Woolmer were central to Kent's encouraging start to the season didn't go unnoticed. 'Kent, who had a tradition of success and wanted to guard it jealously, could not bear the thought of my joining another county and playing against them,' noted Underwood, who'd been approached by Derbyshire captain Eddie Barlow.

In addition to this growing support for Underwood and co, there were the financial aspects to consider. Discussions with lawyers about the potential cost of terminating Packer player contracts, up to £10,000 per player, would have financially crippled the club and with no other county resorting to such drastic action, Kent's general committee began to have second thoughts. On 20 July, after a four-hour meeting, they released a statement acknowledging that it was in the best interests of Kent cricket to offer the Packer players terms after the 1978 season, much to their delight. Underwood, who admitted to feeling the strain, said he looked forward to playing for many years, which is what he'd always wanted to do. He did, however, take legal advice before signing the contract – Kent had stipulated that the Packer players be precluded from playing WSC-style cricket in the UK for a specific number of years – and only signed after the cricket sub-committee threatened at their October meeting to terminate his contract if he hadn't complied by their deadline.

The reprieve didn't please everyone. The letters columns of the local papers were inundated with angry missives from outraged members deploring the onset of player power. Brian Johnston cancelled his Kent membership, accusing the county of putting self-interest before the good of the game. Explaining his position in *The Cricketer* he wrote, 'I do not begrudge them [the players] their understandable desire to ensure their financial future, if that is what they think they have done. But I do not approve of the way they did it, though I agree that it was largely forced on them.

'Apart from the financial situation I also cannot help wondering if they have done the right thing for themselves. What satisfaction can great cricketers like Alan Knott and Derek Underwood get from playing limited-over cricket on football fields under floodlights with a hefty ration of blood and bouncers?'

He thought that the Packer players couldn't expect to have it both ways by being ineligible for England during the winter and expecting to play for Kent in the summer, thereby denying young players such as Downton and Chris Tavaré the chance to prove themselves. (Yet, whatever Johnston's rift with the Packer players, it didn't lead to a permanent estrangement with Underwood, who was a guest at his appearance on *This is Your*

Life in November 1982.) The reprieve also claimed David Clark, who, as president of MCC and chairman of the ICC, felt obliged to resign from the county committee on which he'd served for 30 years.

Although Kent went on to win the Benson and Hedges Cup and the County Championship that season and Underwood took 100 wickets, he found the pressure off the field draining, especially the effect it had on Dawn. 'She knows that whenever we go out, the conversation will turn to cricket. It's always been like that, I know, but I suppose I'm on my guard now, ready for people who only want to knock me for playing WSC.' What particularly upset him was the lack of understanding of what a cricketer's life was like.

He also took issue with those Kent supporters who refused to engage him in conversation and the antipathy of committeemen who belittled his bowling feats during these years. 'I found that attitude small-minded and upsetting,' he wrote in *Deadly Down Under*. 'I look upon those wickets in 1978 and 1979 as being my crowning achievement, yet they were appreciated with muffled gratitude.' Fortunately, he had the support and sympathy of his team-mates which enabled him to forget the arguments and back-biting when out on the field.

After a disappointing first year in which WSC lost a lot of revenue the second year proved more rewarding, since aggressive marketing and more one-day cricket boosted the coffers. In contrast to Australia's 5-1 defeat to England in front of rapidly diminishing attendances, night cricket played on Test match grounds drew vast crowds and greatly increased television ratings. Yet for all the exhilarating nature of the cricket, the winter at times proved torturous for Underwood.

England were touring Australia, and he was playing a rival form of cricket.

During the early part of the Australian season the England party bumped into the WSC players at Sydney airport. Brearley wrote, 'I found the meeting touching in a way, but for Derek it was awkward, even painful.' He would have enjoyed seeing Brearley again but felt embarrassed about phoning him in case the England captain thought it impudent of a Packer player. Acknowledging the lack of pride and identity in a World XI, he missed playing for England. He watched almost every ball of the Ashes series when he wasn't playing and admitted to Alan Lee that, 'There have been times when I would have given a lot to have been out there with them. I've been wanting them to win every Test, and I'll go on wanting England to win for the rest of my days.' Later, at the end of January, it meant a lot to him when Brearley came round to the World XI hotel in Sydney and spent more than two hours discussing the England tour. Underwood later wrote, 'It showed an understanding towards someone with whom he had played for so many years and that I had not been forgotten by my England team-mates. The attitude of one or two England players had been hurtful. They didn't seem to understand that I was only trying to do my best for my wife and children.'

After beginning with a round of one-day games in New Zealand, WSC returned to Australia to play a similar format to the previous year, except a fourth side, the Cavaliers, was added. Beginning with 5-50 against an Australian XI in a one-day game at Perth, Underwood took six wickets, five of them recognised batsmen, against the same opposition in the World XI's 102-run victory in the first Super Test. He also took a valuable 3-68 in their thrashing of West Indies. In a form of cricket in which fast bowlers dominated, he was the only spinner who emerged from WSC with his reputation intact. (In five Super Tests he took 16 wickets at 27.56.) Asked by Andrew Murtagh, Barry Richards' biographer, how he felt he'd coped, he replied with typical modesty, 'Oh, I didn't have much to do. Not with the battery of West Indian fast bowlers in the side. All I had to do was wheel away for a few overs while they had a rest. And when we were playing West Indies, we had Garth le Roux, Imran Khan and Mike Procter to spearhead our attack, although I just provided a bit of variety here and there.'

It was his batting, however, that caught the eye in the Super Test final against the Australians at the SCG. Entering at 104/9 in reply to the home side's 172, he was badly dropped in the gully when on 2. Capitalising on his reprieve, he added 64 with South African fast bowler Garth le Roux and by the time he was bowled by Lillee for 32 they were right back in the game. The Australians were rattled, as Underwood discovered in their second innings when the last-wicket pair of Lillee and Lenny Pascoe were eking out every run. During one over bowled by le Roux to Pascoe, Lillee would stride halfway down the pitch to encourage his partner. On the penultimate delivery, Pascoe pushed the ball to Underwood at mid-off. Noting that Lillee had left his crease and was off chatting to Pascoe, Underwood told him that he could have run him out because the ball wasn't yet dead. Unimpressed with this mildest of rebukes, Lillee saw red, telling Underwood what he thought of him, and he continued to remonstrate with him after Pascoe was bowled next ball. Seeing their team-mate under attack, Mike Procter and Clive Rice came to his rescue and received similar treatment for their pains.

Set 224 to win, the World XI eased home by five wickets owing to an undefeated century from Barry Richards, described as magnificent by Underwood. 'I think he was the most balanced batsman I've ever seen,' he later told Murtagh. 'He seemed to sway either forward or back, depending on length. He was so poised at the crease and had such natural timing. He didn't crunch the ball off the bat, it just flowed. In WSC he stood out even in that illustrious company.'

The game concluded on an acrimonious note. Severely critical of rival captain Tony Greig throughout the summer, Ian Chappell acted churlishly in defeat by shaking everyone's hand except his, a breach of etiquette that didn't meet with Underwood's approval.

It also marked the end of Underwood's participation in WSC because, with both sides losing money, a compromise was reached between the ACB and Packer in May 1979. Looking back at the enterprise many years later he claimed that he never had a moment's regret about signing up. 'It was a decision I made for my family. I also look back on it as a great cricketing experience. There's a nucleus of players like Viv Richards and Gordon Greenidge, with who I share a bond. We were rebels, but we helped cricket progress.' According to Asif, Underwood had a special affinity with Pakistanis. He wrote, 'When WSC came along he had the undisputed portfolio of being our tea maker, a responsibility which he fulfilled with considerable distinction. He would react violently each time he heard the word "Deadly" amidst a lot of Urdu and if WSC had carried on a little longer he would perhaps have ended up by learning the language. But the truth is that I can hardly think of anyone with whom Derek could not get along.'

WSC certainly brought more money into the game, improved pay for all cricketers and pioneered night cricket which attracted a new, wider audience. Conversely, the aggressive marketing, the boorish crowds and decline in sportsmanship weren't to Underwood's liking. Commenting on the Englishmen's attitude to WSC, Barry Richards reckoned they felt a tad uncomfortable. 'Maybe the razzle dazzle was alien to their more conventional, conservative culture. They never really embraced it all in the same way that the laid-back West Indians did.'

Underwood also regretted the disruption caused by WSC and the loss of friendships but remained puzzled by the failure of others to understand the need for financial security. Yet the passage of time quelled much of the bitterness and allowed for a meeting of minds. Geoff Cope, an avid opponent of WSC, recalls going to stay with Underwood at his smart new home at Sevenoaks in the early 1980s and on arrival he said to him, 'So this is Packerville and he replied, "I thought you'd have something to say. Can I talk to you about it?' 'Course you can,' said Cope, "You're a pal." "Do you know," he continued, "by signing up for three years my daughters and my family are secure, and that's the only reason I did it."

'That took a lot of the bitterness away from me,' concluded Cope. 'Here was Deadly saying he did it for his family; it was a pay deal that wouldn't come along again. That gave me a different edge to it.'

Chapter 10

Second Coming

ON 30 May 1979 the great schism which had ruptured the cricket world was finally healed. Deeply in debt, the ACB felt compelled to come to terms with WSC and although they nominally regained the right to run cricket in Australia they found themselves in thrall to the Packer organisation. His Channel Nine network was guaranteed exclusive rights to broadcast and promote cricket in Australia for ten years.

To help the Board restore its ailing finances, England reluctantly agreed to tour there for a second consecutive winter to participate in a triangular one-day international competition with Australia and the West Indies and in a three-Test series against Australia.

While the TCCB accepted the gruelling itinerary – 20 internal flights in 93 days – which was geared towards the interests of television rather than the players, they refused to play for the Ashes in the abbreviated Test series and demanded an additional tour guarantee from the ACB.

As the two boards wrangled over the terms of the tour, Underwood, now eligible to play for England again, staked his claim for a Test recall in a year when Kent slipped from their pedestal. A comprehensive defeat by Middlesex at Canterbury on the final day of the season deprived them of the JPL, the nearest they came to winning a trophy. While the old stagers remained in residence (Knott filled in for the university-educated Downton during the first half of the season), several of them were past their prime and an air of complacency had crept in. In the Championship Underwood was left to shoulder the attack, his 104 wickets more than double the next highest. Even he struggled at first aside from match-winning performances against Gloucestershire and Derbyshire, but by July he was back to his best. Against Nottinghamshire at Folkestone, he caused mayhem on a dampish pitch, finishing with match figures of 13-71. Covering the game for the *Kent Messenger*, their cricket correspondent Stephen Brenkley wrote, 'For two days he proved for the umpteenth time that he has no comparison as a wet-wicket bowler. The conditions suited him perfectly, but he was supreme as always in taking advantage of them. His bounce and turn on the drying pitch ... was perilous as ball after ball reared up at the poor batsmen, some of whom can never have seen such venom before from a medium-pace bowler.'

Quashing speculation that Underwood wasn't the bowler of yesteryear, he continued, 'On pitches that have reputedly offered him no encouragement this season, he might have struggled for wickets but has been more miserly than ever in conceding runs.'

He then decimated Hampshire on a drying pitch at Bournemouth with 8-28 and Glamorgan at Cardiff with 8-88 and 5-14. Kent won both games by an innings and in every one of their six Championship victories that year Underwood was victor ludorum. His success raised the possibility of a Test comeback, a prospect that divided opinion. Denis Compton argued that both principle and planning dictated that Knott, Underwood and Woolmer should remain in the cold. 'I can understand the trio's reasons for having turned their backs on England. The money Kerry Packer paid them – the contracts included this coming winter – went a long way towards establishing their financial security. But they must not be allowed a second bite at the Test cherry. That would mean leaving out players with a more significant part to play in England's future.'

Yet, looking ahead to the formidable challenge awaiting them in Australia, Ted Dexter thought Underwood should tour. 'I believe he is a must, and whatever problems there are about recalling Kerry Packer cricketers, England need all the big guns they can get. Deadly Derek is quite simply the best slow left-armer in the world,' a view that contrasted with his earlier assessment of him.

In Underwood's absence with WSC, England had looked to Middlesex's Phil Edmonds to lead the spin attack. Comparing him to Underwood, Illingworth, who took umbrage against WSC players, wrote, 'He is younger, has better variation, spins the ball more and is a razor-sharp close fielder. He is also a more reliable batsman than his Kent rival.'

His dismissive assessment brought a blistering response from John Shepherd, who noted that Underwood had taken 132 more Test wickets than Illingworth. He wrote, 'All I can imagine is that Raymond has altered his opinion of Underwood for whenever they were faced with a batting track in their England days together Illingworth always put Underwood to the slaughter, saving himself it seemed until the dust began to fly.'

After a promising first year leading the England spin attack, Edmonds lost his place on the 1978/79 tour of Australia and disappointed against India the following summer. On top of that, he had a fractious relationship with Brearley who, as a respected captain, had a decisive say on selection. Always a great supporter of Underwood, he argued that his form that season justified his return. It so happened that the day before the tour party was due to be announced Kent were hosting Middlesex in the JPL and at the end of the game Edmonds approached Underwood in the shower to offer his congratulations. 'Thanks, I don't know what to say,' replied Underwood. Later he wrote, 'I had to admire him for coming and telling me, and thought it said a lot of his strength of character.'

Although delighted by his recall, he fretted about the reaction of his team-mates, some of whom had been strongly critical of the Packer players. His confidence was hardly boosted by Boycott's adverse reaction to Edmonds' omission. 'Underwood will bowl anywhere,' he commented, 'but he can't bat, and his fielding is certainly not equal to Phil's.' His outburst and various domestic problems all contributed to excessive tension, reflected in his high blood pressure at his medical at Lord's prior to departure. He wrote, 'My nerves hadn't been too good at all towards the end of the season, and I still felt strangely unsettled, even after the tour party had been made known. We were moving house too, and I'd had trouble selling my home. I have to admit at times the children got on top of me; I couldn't relax, I was over-emotional and even tearful. I couldn't sleep properly and actually finished up on Valium before we left for Australia, something I'd never resorted to in all my time in cricket.'

He also expressed worry about his mother's health and the continued criticism of him over WSC. An ITN reporter came to his house in Sevenoaks and said, 'If it wasn't for Packer, I don't suppose you would have been able to afford this new house.' Underwood asked that they stick to the cricket and banned photos of his family.

After his pre-tour tribulations, it was a relief to arrive in Australia and be welcomed back by all the team. Following figures of 8-41 in England's opening game against Combined Universities (a non-first-class game), Brearley, having asked him to lead the team off the field, said, 'Well bowled, Deadly, it's good to have you back.' For his part, Underwood was delighted to be playing under Brearley again, since he greatly admired his handling of his players and his dignified reaction to attacks from the Australian media and crowds. When Boycott subjected him to an undiplomatic outburst at practice before the Perth Test over his supposed failure to act on his advice, Underwood later criticised him for undermining his captain.

The tour began in a climate of rancour because of the TCCB's refusal to accept the conditions proposed by the ACB. Not only did they disapprove of the coloured clothing strips, the use of white balls in day matches and restricted field placings, they demanded an additional tour guarantee, all of which fuelled Australian resentment. In the more gladiatorial atmosphere created by WSC the press and home crowds weren't slow to express their hostility, especially towards Brearley. Recalling an incident in a one-day international (ODI) against Australia at the SCG on Boxing Day when Ian Chappell and Dennis Lillee taunted Brearley over a missed run-out, Underwood wrote, 'Lillee and Chappell may have thought they were being funny when they ridiculed Brearley and may have seen their gestures as gamesmanship to goad the crowd into a greater anti-Pom and in particular anti-Brearley mood. But their behaviour was not becoming for two of Australia's most talented cricketers.' Condemning their antics as totally unwarranted, he thought it bizarre that no one in Australian officialdom saw fit to either publicly or privately reprimand them.

Underwood wrote with some feeling because, in the previous ODI against Australia at the SCG, he was struck on the neck by a piece of metal thrown at him. Subjected to constant abuse on the boundary, not least from young boys, he began to wonder whether he should sign their autograph books at close of play. According to Brearley, fielders placed on the boundary were at risk and in a radio interview before the second Test at the SCG he warned that 'someday, somebody is going to be killed in front of an Australian crowd', comments that didn't endear him to the locals.

Underwood also denounced Lillee's display of dissent towards Brearley and the umpires when they objected to the use of his aluminium bat in the Perth Test, a contretemps that ended with Lillee throwing his bat in disgust towards the pavilion. He wrote, 'This was a shocking example for hundreds of adoring young cricket lovers who regarded Lillee as their idol, particularly in Western Australia, where he can do nothing wrong.'

His boorishness aside, Lillee remained a great bowler and was chiefly responsible for England's defeat in the first Test at Perth. They gathered at the SCG at the turn of the year where torrential rain and a saturated pitch prevented a prompt start to the second Test. Conditions were still far from perfect when the umpires called the captains together to ascertain their views. One down in a three-Test series, Brearley was keener to play than his opposite number Greg Chappell, knowing that he had Underwood, the great doyen of drying pitches at his disposal, but as luck would have it, Chappell won the toss and inserted England.

All out for 123, England restricted Australia's lead on first innings to 22, only then to lose three quick wickets on the second evening. Sent in as nightwatchman, Underwood was promised a crate of beer by Botham if he survived to lunch and playing with great resolution, he battled it out with Brearley. 'I enjoyed the experience of batting with Mike, especially in Sydney,' he wrote. 'He is unselfish and the sort of cricketer who will always come down the wicket, say encouraging things, and offer assistance when we are in difficulty.' Receiving several painful blows on the thigh, Underwood would note Brearley's wry smile concealed by his helmet and think to himself, 'There must be easier ways to earn a living.'

With a series of pushes and nudges, the pair added 50 before Brearley was out. Underwood continued to battle away until lunch and when he came off the field Botham was waiting at the dressing room door. Putting his arm around him, he said, 'The beer's been ordered.'

Out in the first over after lunch, Underwood returned to a hero's reception. His 43, his equal second-highest Test score, enabled England to set Australia 219 to win. Capturing the first three wickets, he kept his team in contention before erring in line as Greg Chappell's 98 not out guided Australia to a six-wicket win.

Chappell, so often one of Underwood's victims, asserted his supremacy against him once again in Australia's eight-wicket victory at Melbourne, punishing him in both innings as he tired. According to John Woodcock, he'd never seen him played better than by Chappell or with more calculated aggression, and while

Underwood expressed disappointment with his bowling in the Tests – 11 of his 12 wickets were recognised batsmen – it was the fragility of England's batting that saw them come off a poor second.

Less economical than in the past, Underwood gave way to off-spinner John Emburey in the one-day finals against West Indies, but he kept his place for the Jubilee Test against India at Bombay. For a conventional personality like Underwood, sharing with the irrepressible Botham at the exclusive Taj Mahal Hotel proved at times a gruelling experience. On arrival at Bombay airport, Underwood asked him what they should get for their duty free, to which Botham replied, 'I don't mind as long as there's plenty of it.' Underwood filled the bag with gin and whisky, and when challenged by the customs official over whether he had anything to declare, Botham assured him he had nothing of significance, and they were let through.

Aware of the pride Botham derived from an expensive pair of blue crocodile skin shoes he had purchased in Australia, Underwood told him that if he wanted them looking spic and span he should leave them outside their room. They would be cleaned and returned the following morning. Botham followed his advice but much to his mortification they were never seen again.

Collaborating with the *Daily Mirror*'s Chris Lander on his book about England's time in Australia, Underwood wanted some peace to finish it, but whenever Lander came into their suite Botham would insist on some drinks and if they went to Lander's suite Botham would come and join them. He wrote, 'The more they tried to avoid me, the more relentless I was in my pursuit and after three or four king-size cocktails in the hotel bar neither of them was in good enough shape to get back to work afterwards.'

'One evening, I dragged Deadly and Lander to the restaurant at the top of the hotel. Deadly became so intoxicated that he started dancing and gyrating on a table where a couple were trying to eat their meal. Then Lander joined in with catastrophic consequences, and slipping and landing head-first in the lap of one of the diners. As punishment, I set Deadly and Lander the challenge of standing on a table, drinking a glass of brandy, eating a plate of tandoori chicken and reading a passage from the Gideon Bible, all at the same time. I can report that Deadly was not up to the task.'

For several mornings at breakfast, team-mates would comment on Underwood's bleary appearance and by the final day of their stay he was found asleep on a stranger's floor just to get away from Botham.

Botham's nocturnal activity in no way impaired his brilliance in the Test, his century and 13 wickets resulting in a ten-wicket victory for his side. In addition to admiring his prowess as an all-rounder, Underwood respected his acumen, vitality and team spirit. In *Deadly Down Under*, he commended Botham's claim for the England captaincy, but in India he warned him off it since such a responsibility had ruined many great players.

Underwood's good relationship with Lander was symptomatic of the trust which still existed between players and journalists. He was particularly close to Dudley Moore, the voice of Kent cricket who also happened to be his agent, and he wrote a foreword to his *History of Kent County Cricket Club* published in 1988. According to Stephen Brenkley, Underwood was always willing to discuss the game and never talked down to a scribe. He recalled having dinner with him after Sussex's Kepler Wessels had scored 138 not out against Kent at Tunbridge Wells in 1977, when he spent a full half hour dissecting the way he played, breaking down the batsman's technique.

Mark Baldwin of *The Times*, then working on the *Sevenoaks Chronicle*, was sent by his editor in 1981 to interview Underwood, who'd just received his MBE in the New Year's Honours List, at his home. He wrote in 2024, 'It was, on the face of it, a daunting task for someone not long out of university. But Derek could not have been more welcoming, especially to a green-as-grass young reporter understandably nervous at knocking at the door of one of England's greatest cricketers. Soon I was sitting in his lounge, chatting about all aspects of his career to date and cricket in general; and I remember even now my astonishment that someone so famous in his field could be so generous with his time. He even invited me back again when after an hour's chat over tea and biscuits and with my lengthy list of interview questions still to be exhausted, he announced with regret that he had to pop out to some errands that could not all wait.'

Baldwin derived pleasure from further interviews often over a couple of pints in his local pub. Underwood also once gave his teenage son Jamie a one-to-one coaching session in a deserted all-weather tennis court at the golf club of which they were both members, much to the disbelief of Baldwin's father.

In a damp start to the 1980 season and with few opportunities to bowl, Underwood felt out of practice and rhythm. Picked for the second Test against West Indies at Lord's, he conceded 35 runs in his first six overs and fell victim to an imperious onslaught from Viv Richards, who scored a majestic 145. When he bowled Andy Roberts to claim his sole wicket in the game, it was only his tenth wicket of the season. Lacking his usual control, he was dropped. Out of luck in June and July, he salvaged his season with 6-71 and 6-28 against Essex at Folkestone, a game Kent lost, and 7-78 against Middlesex at Canterbury, where only a superb century from Brearley kept him at bay. In what was a dreadful season for Kent, they slumped to 16th in the Championship, a position they last occupied in 1958, and made limited headway in the limited-overs game. Ealham was stripped of the captaincy and dropped unceremoniously from the side at the beginning of the new season just at a time when the atmosphere in the dressing room began to deteriorate. Aside from the shoddy standards of dress, there was more noise on the field and a growing cynicism among the younger players. 'The attitude was just starting to change,' observed Ealham, 'and Brian [Luckhurst] did get some stick from the younger players. I also remember Derek Underwood being called an old tosser, which really upset him.'

Back to his best in 1981, Underwood enjoyed a golden Canterbury Week, taking 21 wickets in the games against Essex and Hampshire. He also scored his second ever fifty, sharing a ninth-wicket partnership of 108 with debutant Richard Ellison. One flowing cover drive down to the famous lime tree by Ellison so reminded him of Gary Sobers that Underwood called him Sir Garfield Elly.

Thinking that the Old Trafford pitch, venue for the fifth Test against Australia, would take spin, the selectors included him in the 12, only to leave him out on the morning of the game. He hoped for better luck next time round, but it wasn't to be. According to Brearley, 'The following Test was at the Oval, where we knew that the pitch was likely to be fast and bouncy and would probably not favour spinners. So we left Derek out of the 12, though privately we had no doubt that he would be the man we would call on at the last minute if the pitch looked helpful to spinners. Since he had not played in the previous Test, and since he was, in our minds, still our second spinner, if needed, we did not feel he had, in any real sense, been dropped. So, though I phoned Graham Gooch and David Gower to tell them their bad news, I omitted to phone Underwood. Unfortunately, the announcement of the side at Folkestone where Kent were playing their Sunday match made mention only of Gooch's and Gower's replacement by Wayne Larkins and Paul Parker. Everyone congratulated Underwood for keeping his place in the 12 and it was not until his mother phoned him at teatime that he discovered the truth.'

Once again exploiting Folkestone's uneven surface, he took 7-118 off 54.4 overs against Somerset, bowling Viv Richards much to his fury, yet despite his efforts, Kent were soundly beaten. According to off-spinner Vic Marks, 'It had been one of our better performances and I remember it more clearly than most since, for one game only, my figures had matched those of Underwood, one of England's greatest ever spinners, though you would not have guessed this bumping into him at the bar in the pavilion. Underwood hid his prowess and his fierce competitive streak well. Generally, he would be found with a beer in one hand, a fag in the other and a self-deprecating smile on his lips.'

Days later he had plenty to celebrate on gaining his 2,000th wicket at Bournemouth when Graham Johnson caught Hampshire's David Turner. Not only did he become the 32nd bowler to achieve this landmark, following in the footsteps of Kent stalwarts Colin Blythe, Tich Freeman, Frank Woolley and Doug Wright, he will surely be the last of that select band, given the ever-growing reduction of the fixture list. Reviewing his season, Brenkley wrote, 'His ability to attack and harass was always in evidence on any wicket, his unqualified gift for containment a boon once more in the 40-over competition.'

His impressive figures that year gained him selection for England's tour to India and Sri Lanka, especially since the new captain Keith Fletcher – dismissed 20 times by him in his first-class career – rated him very highly. The tour nearly didn't take place because of the Indian government's objection to the presence of Boycott and Geoff Cook, who had both played in the recent past in South Africa. It needed some subtle diplomacy by the TCCB and public statements of their opposition to apartheid by both players to resolve the impasse.

Delighted to be playing under Fletcher, Underwood began the tour in good spirits, buoyed by his 11 wickets against the Board of Control President's XI on a helpful pitch at Nagpur, but thereafter he struggled. India's victory in the first Test at Bombay was followed by five tedious draws as the home side protected their lead on dead pitches. An additional hazard was the size of umpire Swaroop Kishen, who stood in three Tests. By bowling wide of the crease Underwood found him difficult to get round and so he had to straighten his run-up, which proved equally challenging.

The one game that promised a result was the fourth Test at Calcutta. In his most probing spell of the series, Underwood took 3-45 in the first innings, dismissing Gavaskar for the 12th and final time in a Test with a superb delivery. The two previous balls pitched just outside the off stump so when the third ball came down Gavaskar's left foot automatically went in the direction of the leg stump, but this time he was flummoxed by one that pitched on off stump and went straight on. He wrote, 'That was very, very good bowling by Underwood, because this ball was also delivered a little slower than the earlier two deliveries.' Yet according to Gavaskar, who averaged 62.50 in the series, Underwood was a shadow of his former self. 'Although the accuracy was still there, the vital nip off the wicket was often missing.' On a turning pitch in the Madras Test, he was out-bowled by the Indian spinners Ravi Shastri and Dilip Doshi, and his frustration became apparent on the final day when the crowd threw oranges, nuts and other rubbish at him on the boundary. The more exasperated he became the more they baited him until Fletcher replaced him with Botham, who played up to the crowd and won them over.

Underwood's spirits lifted when England moved to Sri Lanka, where they were sumptuously entertained. Playing against the host country in their first Test, he took 5-28 including the wickets of their two half-centurions, Ranjan Madugalle and the 18-year-old Arjuna Ranatunga, who shouldered arms.

Leading by only five runs on first innings, England were then made to sweat in stifling conditions as Sri Lanka, inspired by a dazzling 77 from Roy Dias, closed the third day on 152/3. The next morning, after beginning quietly they lost their last seven wickets for eight runs in a dramatic collapse against Emburey (6-33) and Underwood (3-67) who, according to *The Times*' Richard Streeton, 'showed all the accuracy and cunning of master craftsmen'.

England's target was 171 and with Tavaré scoring a disciplined 85 they won by seven wickets, their first victory overseas for two years, some consolation for an arduous, unfulfilling tour played for the most part on lifeless pitches. In his summary of the trip for *The Cricketer*, Underwood wrote that 'the time-wasting and slow play which dominated the last five Tests should never be allowed to catch hold of the game and would not have been tolerated in England'.

The tour also witnessed the premature return home of Boycott, whose century at Delhi saw him become the leading run-scorer in Test cricket. Unhappy with the accommodation, food and hygiene upcountry, Boycott also took issue with Fletcher's leadership over his public criticism of his rate of scoring and with manager Raman Subba Row over his health requirements. Their rift came to a head during the Calcutta Test when Boycott, recovering from a fever, didn't field in India's second innings and went off to play golf on the final day without permission from the management.

His egregiousness upset his team-mates, and his general depression led to his return home, an unfortunate end to his Test career. Even Underwood, who understood him better than most, afforded him little sympathy on this occasion. He wrote in *The Cricketer*, 'Personally I knew he had health problems: India is not an easy place, but I felt that once he had achieved his ultimate goal, Sobers's Test record, some of the ambition, which has fired him for so long, died.'

He reflected later, 'I had the highest regard for him as a cricketer, and I had a great admiration for his guts and determination. And over all our years together in the Test team I had grown very tolerant, very patient with him. But I must admit what he did in Calcutta did not show much respect for the team.'

Underwood's success in Sri Lanka took him to 297 wickets but knowing his Test career was nearing its end he risked all by joining a rebel tour to South Africa, the first of many to that country during the 1980s.

Ever since 1971 South Africa had been subjected to an international sports boycott, a powerful weapon which helped bring home to them the extent of their isolation. In 1976 the new South Africa Cricket Union was formed to administer multi-racial cricket, but despite the progress made it failed to secure the readmission of South Africa to the ICC or end the boycott, reflected in the 1977 Gleneagles Agreement between Commonwealth countries.

What's more, the 1980/81 England tour of the West Indies had been severely disrupted because of the Guyanese government's objection to seamer Robin Jackman's connections with South Africa and only last-minute diplomacy had saved England's recent tour of India.

Thwarted by the international climate, South Africa now looked to instigate a commercially sponsored tour by a quasi-England team. The idea was first mooted by Boycott and his friend Peter Cook, a South African businessman and cricket enthusiast, on Boycott's holiday to South Africa in December 1980. The month-long tour would be planned to avoid disruption to the international Test schedule or the English domestic season. Six England players – Boycott, Graham Gooch, David Gower, Graham Dilley, Botham and John Emburey – were secretly sounded out about the idea in Guyana during their tour of the West Indies and all of them undertook in principle to join a rebel team.

The proposals suffered a setback when the TCCB, on hearing rumours of a proposed tour of South Africa, wrote to all contracted county players in August, warning that anyone playing cricket there would be banned from playing for England. Consequently, Gower and Botham later pulled out in India, concerned about the loss of earnings from a potential Test ban, leading to the withdrawal of Holiday Inns as sponsors, but Peter Cook wasn't giving up that easily. He unearthed a new sponsor, South African Breweries, and recruited new players such as Dennis Amiss and Alan Knott so that by the time England arrived in Sri Lanka, Underwood, along with four others, signed up, attracted by contracts worth about £40,000 for a month's work. As to the moral and political arguments about playing there, Underwood thought that personal freedom aside, a tour of South Africa could only help build bridges with its cricketing authorities, who'd taken steps to make the game more multi-racial.

On their return home on 24 February, Underwood, Gooch, Lever and Emburey went directly to one of the airport hotels at Gatwick for a pre-arranged meeting with Peter Cook and solicitor Leon Selegson. With TCCB officials in their midst, they refrained from conducting any business at the airport as planned. Instead, the officials visited their homes over the next two days to finalise contracts. In contrast to Bob Willis who now withdrew and Keith Fletcher, who refused to join because of his desire to remain England captain, Boycott, who'd returned early from India and had played little part in recent discussions, signed up at the eleventh hour.

On 28 February, seven of the players – Amiss, Boycott, Emburey, Gooch, Knott, Lever and Underwood – slipped out of London under a cloak of secrecy to travel first class to Johannesburg, where they were joined by Chris Old and Les Taylor, who were already out there. The next day saw the arrival of Mike Hendrick, Wayne Larkins and Peter Willey; later they were joined by Bob Woolmer, Geoff Humpage and Arnie Sidebottom to complete the team, the majority past their prime. Once the news of their arrival was made public the reaction back home was overwhelmingly critical, not least from the trade union movement and the Labour and Liberal parties. The Thatcher government, while accepting the right of sportsmen to visit South Africa, disapproved of the tour; *The Times* denounced the selfish attitude of the cricketers for causing a potential rift within the cricket world along racial lines; *The Guardian* declared they were being bribed to help South African apartheid; Mike Brearley refuted Gooch's claim that they were in South Africa simply to play cricket and the TCCB urged them to reconsider their position given the risk to the international game. In Kent Keith Speed, MP for Ashford, thought the trip ill-advised and his Labour opponent Paul Lewis said the rebels had given comfort to one of the world's most brutal regimes; consequently, Knott, Underwood and Woolmer should never play for their county again. From a playing perspective, Kent manager Brian Luckhurst, while understanding of professionals seeking financial security, couldn't condone the trip because of the damage it would cause to the game at large, whereas Colin Page, now director of youth coaching, damned the political reaction, remarking, 'Gleneagles is a place for playing golf.'

With the cricket boards of India and Pakistan, under pressure from their governments, threatening to call off their tours of England that summer, the TCCB on 19 March imposed a three-year ban on the South Africa rebels. The severity of the ban shocked them although Underwood was more philosophical than most, stating that they had gone into it with their eyes open, a view akin to that of Christopher Martin-Jenkins, editor of *The Cricketer*. He wrote, 'Those who finally chose to go to South Africa at the beginning of March knew that they were playing with fire. They had every legal right to go to South Africa and we should not necessarily condemn them, but they were naive and stubborn to ignore the consequences.'

In contrast to the hostility back home, the reception was much more favourable in South Africa, but the cricket itself was something of an anti-climax. Confronted with an arduous schedule of three ODIs and three four-day 'Tests' against a strong South Africa side in a month, Gooch's men under-performed. Soundly defeated in all three ODIs, they were trounced in the first 'Test' by eight wickets and drew the other two games amid waning public interest. With most of the party under-performing – Underwood managed only five wickets all tour – and little obvious benefit to the wider game in South Africa, the tour failed from both a cricketing and commercial point of view. 'It is not a glorious chapter in their history. They ought not to tell their children that they came,' commented Desmond Tutu, Archbishop of Cape Town and leading civil rights activist.

The tour posed a predicament for the Kent committee. Meeting on 30 March, chairman John Pocock suggested there were three options open to them about how they dealt with Knott, Underwood and Woolmer. These were: to pass a resolution that they should be allowed to continue to play for Kent; to do nothing (which would have the same effect); or to negotiate with them a severance package. After discussion they resolved by ten votes to eight that the players concerned should be allowed to continue to play for Kent, but they should also be made aware of the committee's extreme displeasure at their actions.

A week later the chairman and other leading club figures met with the three players to express their opposition to the tour, citing the difficulties it had posed to international and county cricket, and wholeheartedly backed the TCCB ban. Admitting it would be too costly to sack them, they offered the players the three choices they'd previously agreed to in committee. The players, surprised at the committee's hostile reaction, considered the matter and opted to continue to play for Kent.

In line with a TCCB agreement that none of the rebels should play against India and Pakistan that summer, the three players were omitted from the Kent side that played the Indians in May, a decision that led to a boycott of the game by many members and the smallest crowd seen at Canterbury for years.

In another year of under-achievement by Kent – they finished 13th in the County Championship – Underwood easily topped the county bowling averages. He began in fine fettle, not least his 7-79 against Hampshire at Bournemouth, only then to see his standard lowered by Middlesex's Mike Gatting at Tunbridge Wells. The latter wrote, 'I found myself hitting all these sixes over long-off or long-on against "Deadly" Underwood and they sailed into the rhododendron bushes round the ground. It was quite a quick hundred that I got, and I can still see these mauve-coloured rhododendrons and "Deadly" standing there with his little fists clenched at his side, saying, "If I hadn't flipping well bowled at you in the nets in India, you wouldn't have been able to do that!" It was probably the first time I'd ever felt at home against Underwood's bowling.' According to Christopher Cowdrey, Middlesex were the one team to go after him, with Gatting and Clive Radley leading the way, but while they had some triumphs, no side ever completely mastered him.

Away from the cricket Underwood gave greater priority to his growing family. In February 1976 their first child, Heather, was born, followed by Fiona in November 1977, two days after he had departed for Australia to play in WSC. Because he was away so much during the girls' early years the onus fell on Dawn to create a normal, happy household, something at which she succeeded admirably. On one occasion as the girls were coming out of school, Fiona turned to her and said, 'Mummy, why is Daddy's photo in the paper?'

A loving, affectionate father, Underwood enjoyed a warm relationship with the girls, reading and playing games with them and by protecting them from undue publicity he enabled them to lead happy, normal lives.

In 1979 the Underwoods moved to a lovely house in Sevenoaks, a convenient commuting centre with excellent schools and close to Knowle Park, ideal for family outings. Christmas 1980 was Underwood's first at home for five years and he much appreciated spending it with family, friends and his dogs. A consummate host along with Dawn, who was a superb cook, they entertained in style, most notably a joint 40th birthday party. Although not domesticated, he enjoyed gardening and took good care of the family finances. Reading the *Financial Times* on Saturdays, he studied intently his stocks and shares and with expert advice he invested wisely.

In November 1980 Underwood received a letter from the Prime Minister's Office. Dawn knew immediately its content: her husband had been awarded the MBE and she put the champagne on ice while he visited his mother to let her in on the secret; then on his return he was serenaded with Cliff Richard's 'Congratulations'.

Several months later, on 24 February, Underwood, dressed in top hat and tails, and accompanied by his family, was chauffeured to Buckingham Palace in a new Rolls-Royce to receive his honour from the Queen. The fact that the investiture coincided with the announcement of Prince Charles's engagement to Lady Diana Spencer only added to the allure of the occasion.

Touring with England again the following winter, Underwood took the whole family to India, one of their highlights being a visit to the Taj Mahal. Weeks later he was only too delighted to have them with him in South Africa to offset some of the flak associated with this unsanctioned tour. Able to see more of her husband than normal, Dawn counted this trip as one of her most enjoyable, the last one he went on in England colours, albeit in an unofficial capacity.

Chapter 11

Elder Statesman

MIKE DENNESS was right. The retirement of Les Ames had unfortunate ramifications for Kent cricket, since he was the one man who could keep the committee in check. Cricket committees were notoriously feudal at that time – one thinks of Yorkshire's abrupt dismissal of Championship-winning captain Brian Close in 1970, which chairman Brian Sellers later admitted was the biggest mistake of his life – and the way Kent treated their players post-Denness proved equally insensitive.

It is true that WSC presented the committee with a real dilemma given the strong emotions it aroused on all sides, but the manner of Asif's removal as captain caused lingering hurt. Others to be summarily cast aside included John Shepherd, Graham Johnson, Kevin Jarvis, Alan Ealham and Chris Tavaré (the last two as captain) – all great servants of the club – with little thought for their personal welfare. Underwood felt particularly sore about the departure of Shepherd, who went on to give three years' unstinting service to Gloucestershire, his first century ironically coming against Kent, but only spoke out following his retirement when he criticised the dismissal of Jarvis and others. Concerned that the club's expectations had become too inflated following the successes of the 1970s, he stated they were getting rid of players prematurely.

With other counties such as Middlesex, Somerset and Essex stronger outfits than previously, the path to the summit in the 1980s proved steeper, but the internal dissension did little to raise dressing room morale.

As the great side of the 1970s began to break up Underwood remained like a sturdy oak, a permanent landmark on a changing landscape. A jacket and tie man rather than tracksuit and trainers, he shunned the new fitness culture that became fashionable in the 1980s. On one occasion when he had been dragooned into a run, he took a short cut to the pub where he watched his perspiring team-mates slog it out in the closing stages. Convinced that fitness had assumed an importance out of all proportion to basic skills – 'It is skill not calisthenics, which wins matches,' he stated in Dudley Moore's history of Kent cricket – he had it written into his contract that he would be exempt from pre-season training.

Wedded to his traditional preparation for a day's play of a cup of tea and cigarette, his reliance on tobacco was such that on a quicker-than-anticipated visit to the crease he had to give his packet of cigarettes and matches to the umpire. When thrown into the bath to mark his last day in first-class cricket his only concern was to prevent his cigarettes and matches from getting wet.

For all the occasional clash of priorities, Knott and Underwood were heroes to the new generation of Kent players who'd grown up on the glories of the 1970s. 'Great players, and even better people,' recalled opener Neil Taylor. 'If Deadly spoke, you listened.' What particularly struck him was how meticulously the old stagers prepared for a day's cricket. He recalled arriving at Mote Park, Maidstone, where Kent were playing Lancashire, and seeing Knott and Underwood, with the help of team-mate Mark Benson, a left-handed batsman, in the nets concocting a plan to counter the plethora of left-handers in the opposition line-up. Their diligence soon paid off when almost immediately opener Graeme Fowler was out, stumped Knott bowled Underwood.

Steve Marsh, who had the unenviable task of succeeding Knott behind the stumps in 1986, found it quite daunting keeping to Underwood, but buoyed by his encouragement and compliments – not to mention his accuracy – it soon became a pleasure.

Simon Hinks, a left-handed opener who made his debut in 1982, was another who felt elevated by Underwood's presence. 'It was a great honour to play in the same side as Deadly and Knotty,' he remarked. 'It was impossible not to learn from them.' What impressed him was the way Underwood kept everything so simple. He hadn't changed his game much and advised others to do the same, in addition to working hard.

Although Underwood was not one to grandstand in the dressing room, Taylor recalled how he instilled in the youngsters an awareness of what being a professional cricketer entailed, not least the way they treated their supporters. If they were pleasant to people, he stressed, it could open doors for them.

It was a point reiterated by swing bowler Richard Ellison, who won fame against Australia in 1985. 'Players like Derek Underwood always emphasised that the supporters came to watch you play and to be part of your life and cricket. It's important you let them in.'

Not only did Underwood help Ellison settle in the dressing room and dispense gentle advice when he was bowling, he had him to stay at his Sevenoaks home when Kent played at Tunbridge Wells. Very keen on the etiquette of the game, Underwood disliked gratuitous encouragement, once saying to Ellison, 'Why are you telling me to keep going? I've only bowled one ball.' The other comment that really annoyed him was 'Well bowled, Deadly,' to a regulation straight ball, suggesting that it was his best delivery.

The one occasion when he fell short of the standards he espoused, was his failure to walk for a caught behind against Warwickshire. When umpire Barry Dudleston later berated him for standing his ground, he replied, 'I got done out of ten wickets last year. It's the way the game has gone.' Although appreciative of the added remuneration now available to players, Underwood thought that the greater role money played in the game had made players more selfish and the pressures more intense. And this from someone who always lived in fear of whether he was good enough to play for Kent. Pondering with Mike Brearley why anyone should want to be captain, he said, 'Cricket has put enough strain on me. I'm sure my game would suffer if I became captain.'

With many talented players still on their books, Kent could be forgiven for thinking that the good times would soon return, but although they remained competitive, especially in the one-day game, they'd lost the art of winning. In 1983 they reached the final of the NatWest Bank Trophy (as the Gillette Cup was now called) against Somerset on the back of victories over Essex, Warwickshire and Hampshire. Omitting their regular opener Neil Taylor, the new captain Chris Tavaré elected not to bowl

Underwood in a game reduced to 50 overs because of a delayed start. The all-seam attack bowled well and restricted Somerset to 193/9, but the Kent innings lost momentum against the off-spin of Vic Marks and went down to defeat by 24 runs. The fact that Marks and fellow spinner Viv Richards conceded a mere 58 runs from 19 overs seemed to compound the folly of not bowling Underwood, a man in prime form and with an impeccable record in Lord's finals.

In a better year for Kent in the Championship – they rose six places to seventh – he bowled 909 overs, over 300 more than the next Kent bowler, and took 100 wickets in a season for the tenth time. Somerset's Peter Roebuck, who scored a marathon 99 against him at Maidstone, wrote, 'My experience at the crease was dominated by another duel with Underwood. He is a pitiless bowler, stamping in ball after ball and rejoicing at every wicket. He gives you nothing at all, simply fires the ball at middle and leg and straightens it up off the pitch, trying to coax an edge. Occasionally, he holds one back and every now and then he bowls down a fast yorker but mostly he nags at the batsman's defence, hammering away like ancient warriors besieging a castle.'

Among his most notable performances was his ten wickets in the match against Middlesex at Dartford, including all six in the second innings in a vain attempt to deny the opposition victory. One statistical quirk in that game concerned Middlesex batsman Wilf Slack, who was twice stumped Knott bowled Underwood, lifting his back foot on both occasions.

Several weeks later at Trent Bridge Underwood displayed remarkable stamina for a 38-year-old, bowling 70 overs in the game for his 13-161, helping Kent to a five-wicket victory.

He put in another marathon effort to take seven wickets in each innings against Warwickshire in Canterbury Week, but Kent could only draw; then on a helpful pitch at Folkestone he bowled his side to a ten-wicket victory over Leicestershire with 7-55, his prize victim being Brian Davison, whom he bowled for nought. Finishing with 105 Championship wickets at 19.27, Underwood rated that achievement as one of his most satisfying. 'A few myths were destroyed that season,' he commented. 'It showed that I could do the job on dry, covered pitches as well. That meant a lot.'

At the end of the season, he travelled to New Zealand in some style to represent an International XI in one 50-over game against the home nation. Given the opportunity to go fishing at Rotorua, notable for its geysers, he caught a 3lb trout and when Gatting caught one, too, it was served with herbs and honey after the game, much to their satisfaction.

With the onset of covered wickets in 1980, Underwood hadn't bowled on a rain-affected one for five years, but against Hampshire at Canterbury on 29 May he relived his youth with an awesome display. After the loss of nearly two days' play to the weather some bartering between the two captains Chris Tavaré and Nick Pocock was necessary to secure any chance of a result. Kent batted on before declaring, Hampshire forfeited their first innings and Kent forfeited their second innings, leaving the latter 180 to win in a minimum of 59 overs. According to Hampshire's Mark Nicholas, Pocock returned to the dressing room in a chipper mood. Having seen his seamers get little out of the pitch he was convinced he'd extracted a favourable deal from his opposite number, whereupon experienced batsman David Turner asked him if he'd ever faced Underwood on a wet pitch. Pocock said he hadn't, but the plan was simple: they would block him and score off Terry Alderman and Richard Ellison at the other end. Turner's team-mate Trevor Jesty then asked him if he'd ever blocked Underwood on a turning pitch. 'No,' he answered, 'but it can't be so difficult that we don't make 180 off the others.'

Entering the attack in the fifth over, Underwood began with a maiden before administering his version of waterboarding. After dismissing opener Chris Smith, taken at slip off a brute of a ball that caught the shoulder of his bat, Nicholas took guard and replaced the divot. He wrote, 'The close field was five-strong: two slips, gully, silly point and forward short leg. I figured the best thing was to play back. The ball went past my chest and was taken by Alan Knott at his shoulder height. "Well bowled, Del," said the great stumper. "Thanks, matey," said the great bowler, the two of them in perfect harmony. Knott and Underwood, Underwood and Knott: it occurred to me that I was the piggy-in-the-middle of a collaboration in genius.

'The third ball of the over hit the splice of my bat, heavy and hard. The thing about Underwood was the speed of the ball – almost medium pace and spinning like a top, which gave it the impression of something deadly – thus Deadly. That, and the relentless accuracy. People said he cut the ball, but he didn't really, he spun it at a cutter's pace. The fourth ball of this second over was really evil. Spitting with intent, it attacked the thumb of my right glove, tearing it away from the handle of the bat before it carried on an inevitable path to the poker-faced captain at second slip. He threw it up like a child flicks a Smartie to its lips.'

Nicholas had just made it back to the dressing room when he looked out from the balcony to see Jesty inch forward to another of those lethal deliveries only to find his gloves in the way of a cricket ball that was programmed to travel from hand to pitch, to bat or glove, and on to slip. 'It was a kind of magic, beautiful in its performance, brutal in its effect, irresistible in its result.'

Having seen off Hampshire for 56, Underwood returned to haunt them at Bournemouth, traditionally a spinner's paradise and scene of many a past triumph. Following his 4-34 in the first innings he bowled unchanged in the second as the home side chased 223 for victory on a worn pitch. Although they battled hard, they ultimately fell prey to Underwood who finished with 8-87 off 42 overs, Kent winning by 44 runs.

Appropriately enough it was at Hastings, his cricketing nirvana, that Underwood chalked up his proudest achievement, one that began in the most unpromising of circumstances. On the evening of Saturday, 30 June, he strode to the wicket in his familiar guise as nightwatchman to stem the losses on a day in which 21 wickets had fallen. Resolute as ever, he survived to stumps with Kent 22/1, 30 behind Sussex.

After bowling Kent to a decisive win over Sussex the next day with 6-12, his best figures in the JPL, becoming the second bowler to reach 300 wickets in that competition (John Lever beating him by 15 minutes), he returned to the crease on Monday morning. In overcast conditions with the ball seaming all over the place and against an attack comprising Garth le Roux, Colin Wells, Dermot Reeve and Ian Greig, the Kent upper order sank without trace. Yet amid the carnage Underwood stood firm, launching a savage assault on the redoubtable le Roux, *The Guardian* correspondent reporting that 'his drives through cover invoked the image of a man batting with a crutch'. 'The harder we tried the worse we bowled to Underwood,' wrote Sussex captain Johnny Barclay, 'too many attempted yorkers which he stabbed out and bouncers which he flayed quite successfully. But not enough of the good length balls that had flummoxed the top order.' Having scored 50 out of 65 – Tavaré scored one run in a stand of 44 – he received solid support from Knott and number ten Alderman, whose 52 not out was by some way his career-best. 'I got very nervous,' recalled Underwood. 'I'd made an eighty early in my career, but Kevin Jarvis was our number eleven; and he really couldn't bat. So I thought I'd be left not out, short of the ton.'

Caught off a no-ball, he promptly hit Wells for three fours and after being dropped by Barclay at slip on 92, he pulled Wells to the boundary to reach his maiden century. 'The unconfined delight as he acknowledged the congratulatory toasts of his peers was a joy to behold and to cherish,' wrote the *Daily Telegraph*'s Doug Ibbotson – 'something that cannot be expressed in a mere statistic.' (Underwood reached his century in his 618th innings; only Bob Taylor at the 744th attempt took longer.)

Underwood eventually fell to Reeve for 111 and Kent were bowled out for 243, the match later ending in a tie. His century was one of the real highlights of his career and gave him more satisfaction than just about anything else. 'Even with the applause round the ground and in the dressing room afterwards, it didn't really sink in,' he recalled. 'I suppose the full impact only hit me the next morning when I read about it in the papers. After 22 years it was well worth waiting for.' The century also helped restore domestic harmony. That morning, he and Dawn had had a row and so when a friend rang Dawn at lunchtime to tell her that Derek was on the cusp of a century, she put any lingering hurt to one side to welcome him home.

His season, however, was marred by a second successive defeat in the NatWest Bank Trophy final at Lord's. The previous year, when Underwood hadn't bowled in the final, team-mates joked that he was in the side for his batting; now in the 1984 final against Middlesex after Kent had made 232/6 in their 60 overs, he'd reduced his opponents to a near standstill, his nine overs costing a mere 12 runs and comprising the vital wicket of Roland Butcher. Commenting on his duel with Clive Radley, Middlesex team-mate Simon Hughes wrote, 'It was a mesmerising, old-fashioned sort of duel between the two virtuosos who had the utmost respect for each other. Underwood shuttled up to the wicket, varying his flight to a man who weaved giddily up and down the wicket trying to upset his rhythm.'

In removing him from the attack after nine overs, Tavaré's idea was to save him for the final shootout, but when he returned the batsmen were well set and he didn't pose quite the same threat. 'I couldn't understand why they took Derek off,' remarked Radley after the game. 'Everything seemed to get easier when the others bowled.' Adding 87 in 15 overs with Paul Downton, he put Middlesex back in contention and they won off the last ball in the gloaming by six wickets. It was a disappointing end to an encouraging season in which Kent had climbed to fifth in the Championship, but it wasn't enough to save Tavaré's job as captain. Although experiencing a dip in his own form, he had captained the side with quiet authority and brought people together, but he fell victim to the whims of the Swanton faction on the committee. According to manager Luckhurst, who wasn't consulted about Tavaré's deposition, it was the worst decision that the county had made since the war and it made for an awkward inheritance for Tavaré's successor, Christopher Cowdrey.

Facing an atmosphere of disgruntlement in the dressing room, exacerbated by the controversial sacking of Graham Johnson mid-season, Cowdrey's load was lightened by the support he received from Underwood, despite the occasional difference over his captaincy. Cowdrey recalls Underwood's intense irritation when Cowdrey asked him to toss the ball up to keep Lancashire interested in a fourth-innings run chase at Old Trafford. He ended with figures of 2-93 from 20 overs in a game that Kent won by 25 runs. When they arrived at Chelmsford later that evening to play Essex, a still unhappy Underwood said to Cowdrey, 'I'll see you in the bar,' whereupon they talked through their differences and although they didn't agree – 'Never ask me to do that again,' he said, shaking his head – they respected each other's point of view. 'Whatever happened today is history,' concluded Underwood. 'I'll back you all the way tomorrow against Essex. Let's forget it.'

He was of course as good as his word, leading Cowdrey to call him a 'Captain's dream. Always trying, always advising and never moaning.' In Underwood's 1986 benefit brochure he wrote, 'In the ten years I have been at Kent he has hardly changed at all. On the morning of a home match, he will hurry into the dressing room, normally a few minutes late, wearing the smart grey trousers and blue shirt that he wore in his first benefit year.

'Once the game starts, he can't wait for a bowl, "you can't get wickets unless you bowl" being one of his favourite comments. When put on, he still has the enthusiasm and will to succeed that he has had for over 20 years. His first ball is invariably on the spot, and he will warm to the task, whatever the situation, whatever the wicket. He loves bowling. That near miss when instinctively he raises his left arm like a photographer about to take a picture. The anguish on his face when he is hit to the boundary, the purposeful walk back to his mark when he knows he is on top, and the brilliant and boyish grin that appears when he gets a wicket. He loves bowling.

'There is no doubt that Derek is the best left-arm spinner that I have ever seen. Bishan Bedi displayed remarkable deception in the flight of the ball, and Phil Edmonds in aggression and variation, but Deadly can bowl well on any wicket. On a turner the batsman has little chance of survival, and on a wet wicket he has none. This is why he is the best.' He used to tease Underwood by reminding him that he was greatly in debt to the Cowdrey clan – Colin, Graham and himself – for all the catches they'd taken off his bowling. (Christopher took 65 and Colin 63.)

Now that the three-year South Africa rebel ban had run its course, Underwood harboured hopes that he might play for England again and was delighted when he was picked for MCC against the Australians in 1985. 'This is fantastic news,' he commented. 'Throughout the ban, I was hoping there could be a resumption of my Test career.' The occasion, however, didn't go according to plan. Australia captain Allan Border hit him for three sixes and although Underwood eventually bowled him it was his only wicket at a cost of 93 runs. He fared little better against the Australians when playing for Kent, his two wickets being lower-order batsmen. Although Kent's leading wicket-taker for the 15th time, it wasn't a vintage season, aside from his usual bounty at Dartford where he claimed ten wickets against Essex, and eight wickets against Somerset in the final game at Canterbury.

The game marked the retirement of Knott after the recurrence of an ankle injury which had incapacitated him at the end of the previous season. Still a top-flight performer behind the stumps, he would be greatly missed by one and all, none more so than the bowler off whom he'd taken 107 catches and made 54 stumpings for Kent. 'He is the best wicketkeeper-batsman England has ever produced and certainly the best wicketkeeper I have ever seen,' Underwood said in tribute.

Knott's retirement gave him premonitions of his own mortality. 'The boys were very kind,' he commented, 'but it makes you feel a little lonelier when you're 40 and the next person in the side is probably about 30. They wouldn't want me to see that they've got a bird on their arm, for instance.' As senior professional he noted the demise of the reverential respect that he and his generation had for Colin Cowdrey. 'The younger boys would say, "Morning Deadly" and I was quite comfortable with that, though perhaps 30 years ago it wouldn't have been acceptable.'

In 1986 Underwood was granted a second benefit, a privilege accorded to only four former Kent stalwarts: Frank Woolley, Les Ames, Godfrey Evans and Doug Wright. Unlike his previous benefit Underwood, with no winter tour intervening, had time to prepare it and spent much of it designing his benefit brochure, an improvement on the two previous winters when he'd commuted to London to work for a firm of law stationers. With the popular Derek Ufton, Kent's former wicketkeeper, in charge of the benefit committee and learning from the experience of his previous benefit, Underwood found this one to be much more enjoyable. At one dinner dance near Dover in late August, he was still active on the dance floor in the small hours and at no cost to his cricket, since the next day he took 7-11 against Warwickshire at Folkestone.

Once again, the Great Danes Hotel acted as the launch for his benefit programme, this time a lunch for 300, at which Christopher Martin-Jenkins lauded him as a loyal and thorough professional who, to his knowledge, had never said anything demeaning about anybody. 'He is the most reliable man both on and off the field.'

John Nye, a close friend of the Underwoods, recalls driving him around the villages to play darts in the local pubs and draw the winners in the bat raffles. 'Right, John, I'm just going to circulate,' he would say, and he did it brilliantly.

One novel idea Underwood dreamed up was creating an autographed scroll of all the 65 team-mates he'd played with at Kent. Six of them had migrated to South Africa, four of them to Cape Town – Tony Catt, Ted Fillary, Stuart Leary and Bob Woolmer – and Underwood thoroughly enjoyed catching up with old friends and getting them to contribute to the scroll.

In addition to darts tournaments and dinner dances, there was the usual round of benefit matches – Colin Cowdrey played with sons Christopher and Graham for a Kent XI against Datchet – and a sporting gala dinner was organised by the *Sevenoaks Chronicle* in recognition of his cricketing exploits. The former England batsman Colin Milburn, who shared a room with him on his Test debut, spoke warmly of the universal respect he commanded in the game. It was that respect that helped him to a benefit of £117,120, easily a county record, and the fourth-highest overall to that point.

Two years later Chris Tavaré's benefit committee tried to get Milburn to speak at a dinner. He didn't come cheap and when his various demands for first-class travel and accommodation as well as a hefty fee proved unaffordable Underwood saved the day by inviting him to stay, an invitation Milburn was only too delighted to accept. John Nye recalls driving them home after the dinner and being riveted as they recalled past exploits over a nightcap.

In a wet start to the 1986 season, Underwood featured little in the wickets column as he once again struggled in the Championship. En route to Edinburgh to play against Scotland in the NatWest Bank Trophy, he lost his airline ticket at Heathrow and had to be issued with another one; he then slept through the fire alarm in the team hotel and emerged on the morrow to bowl his 12 overs for 17 runs. Kent won easily but were knocked out of the competition in the next round by Worcestershire three days before they faced Middlesex in the Benson and Hedges Cup final. Playing in his tenth Lord's final, Underwood survived an early onslaught from Clive Radley, who hit him for three fours in one over. As he snatched his jersey at the end of it, Radley asked him whether he would write a piece for his benefit brochure, to which Underwood told him to get lost. Two days later, a lovely tribute appeared in the post.

Radley made 53 but Underwood conceded only 36 runs in his 11 overs in Middlesex's 199/7 in their 55 overs. Requiring 200 to win, Kent endured a faltering start and although a plucky 58 from Graham Cowdrey kept them in contention, they lost by two runs, their third close cup defeat in succession. Reviewing their season to date, John Evans wrote in the *Maidstone Telegraph*, 'The Great Deadly can still contain, as often as not, but he is not winning at 41, as he did at 31 and 21.' He even suffered some punishment from the Lancashire batsmen in his benefit game at Canterbury, where a large Sunday crowd, having listened to a tribute to him from E.W. Swanton, contributed £955 to his collection.

Still without a match-winning performance Underwood looked to Folkestone, one of his favourite grounds, to end his season on a high note. First up were Championship favourites Essex, who won the toss and took first use of a pitch they knew wouldn't last. Underwood claimed three early victims but by the time he had Gooch lbw for 74, Essex had mounted a respectable recovery. 'Our plan was to sit on Deadly Derek and make him bowl a lot of overs, if necessary, which he did, notching up 40 during our first innings, to finish with 4-96,' wrote all-rounder Derek Pringle, who scored an invaluable 97. During the closing overs of the first day, he smote Underwood high towards the midwicket boundary off a no-ball, but Neil Taylor, not hearing the call, raced around the boundary, hurled himself forward and claimed a low diving catch before disappearing over one of the advertising boards. It was an incident which brought a smile to one and all.

Essex's first innings of 280 gave them a platform to control the game and their 50-run victory went a long way towards securing them the Championship.

Warwickshire, in contrast, wilted in similar conditions. Facing a first-innings deficit of 95, they took defence to excess in their endeavours to save the game, all grist to the mill of Underwood and his cordon of close-in fielders. Christopher Cowdrey took five catches off him – emulating Ealham's feat on the same ground 20 years earlier – and the master craftsman ended with the astounding figures of 35.5-29-11-7. Even then he wasn't entirely satisfied, berating himself for bowling one loose delivery which had been hit for four.

With Terry Alderman returning to Australia and Graham Dilley moving to Worcestershire, the Kent attack lacked the depth to challenge for honours in the Championship and they pinned their hopes on the one-day competitions. Defeated in the Benson and Hedges Cup semi-final by Northamptonshire, they once again travelled to Edinburgh to play Scotland in the first round of the NatWest Bank Trophy. Severe weather compelled a late start and on winning the toss Cowdrey duly inserted the home side who faced a searching examination, the type of which their batsmen had never faced before. During the heavy overnight rain, water had seeped under the covers at Myreside, home of Watsonians Cricket Club, and saturated a patch on a length at the Pavilion End. Umpire John Holder, who oversaw Underwood at his end, recalled the danger he posed once he found his line. He wrote, 'With the ball leaping from a length and turning viciously, the Scots were fending it off their throats with all the Kent fielders crouching like vultures, waiting to grab every edge. Honestly, it was one of the most remarkable spells of bowling I have ever witnessed.'

Underwood's 8-31 not only won him his first man of the match award he also beat Alan Dixon's bowling record of 7-15 in the competition (only for Derbyshire's Michael Holding to beat it the following year with 8-24 against Sussex) but Kent's progress in the NatWest was abruptly terminated by Derbyshire in the second round.

In contrast to his success up north, Underwood had lost some of his aura in the Championship, not helped by the modern vogue for grassy wickets. 'I'd have loved to have gone out with 100 wickets, but I barely get a bowl now,' he complained. 'I no longer feel regarded as an attacking bowler. Hard, dry pitches are what groundsmen are supposed to prepare but how often do we see them now? The directive came to them in 1983, and I took 100 wickets that year. So did John Emburey and Norman Gifford. Look at it now.'

In August, having taken 5-43 against Middlesex at Canterbury, his best return of the season, Underwood announced his retirement. It didn't come entirely as a surprise. In March, admitting to weary legs at the end of the previous season, he hinted that this one might well be his last and he opted out of the JPL to preserve his energy for the Championship. Now with advancing years finally catching up with him, he resolved to call it a day at the end of the season. 'I could still churn out the overs in the Championship, though I found that I was struggling physically the day after, but it was the fielding which became a nightmare,' he later reflected. 'Batsmen just used to drop the ball and run, and I thought to myself, five or ten years ago I might have saved that single. Or they used to push it past you. "Look for two, it's Deadly." That was like a knife in the back. So that was the major reason for calling it a day. You couldn't afford to go for runs as well as give them away in the field.'

Such was Underwood's professionalism that even in his final games he continued to give everything to the cause, as Vic Marks recalls: 'He was still bowling his heart out, sweating profusely inside his dirty flannels, chastising himself if he bowled a loose delivery and still striving desperately for just one more wicket for his beloved county.'

The end came in the Championship game against Leicestershire at Canterbury on 12, 14 and 15 September. Friends and relations gathered to witness his farewell, including his nephew Kevin, whose headmaster willingly gave him time off school to witness such a historic occasion. Underwood led the team out on the first morning to a rapturous reception and every time he fielded the ball a deafening cheer would go up from the Kent faithful. Although not at his most devastating, his 32 overs yielded him four more victims including England batsmen Peter Willey and David Gower. Defying the onset of autumn, large numbers continued to turn out on the Monday and Tuesday to bid farewell to one of Kent's greatest cricketers. It wasn't just his dedication, his durability and his unique brilliance, it was the way he played the game and conveyed its finest traditions to players and supporters alike. In an age when corrosive gamesmanship and inflated egos had become commonplace, Underwood combined his fierce determination to win with an engaging modesty that touched everyone who encountered him.

Leading the side out on that final morning to a standing ovation, he toiled away as he had done for 25 years and although a flat pitch denied him any favours, the fierce determination, the nagging accuracy and the subtle changes of pace remained conspicuous to the very end. When the Leicestershire declaration came, and Underwood took his leave to another rousing reception, it marked the end of the era. Alluding to his retirement and that of Dennis Amiss, Woodcock called them 'thrifty, dedicated, tireless and ambitious. If they had their time over again, I doubt whether they would have joined World Series Cricket, but they came through even that with the respect of their friends and with their own respect for the game intact.'

Swanton singled out Underwood's dedication and sportsmanship and in a heartfelt tribute in the *Kent Club Annual*, Les Ames wrote, 'The mere fact that Derek has retired is a sad enough thought, but for it to coincide with a time when the Kent bowling has never been weaker makes it doubly so.'

Calling him the greatest left-arm bowler on a turning wicket the game had ever seen, he compared him with Frank Woolley. 'Batting apart, they had much in common; both were magnificent left-hand bowlers, and both were fine gentlemen on and off the field and a great credit to the game itself.'

Chapter 12

'The Best'

THE EX-ENGLAND batsman Derek Randall once said, 'As soon as you finish playing you get old very quickly.' No longer committed to a disciplined regime of physical fitness, many cricketers, like other sportsmen, lose their sense of motivation and put on weight. Having reached the height of fame by their early 30s, it is a gentle slide into relative obscurity thereafter, so that even for Underwood, who remained trim and fit and a highly venerable figure, it was never, in the words of Robert Browning, 'Glad, confident morning again'.

According to Graham Johnson, who pursued a successful career in business post-cricket, Underwood, once he retired, never found anything as meaningful to replace it. A man of order and routine, he missed the regimented life of a first-class cricketer and its easy access to his many friends. Selling pitches, coaching youngsters and speaking at club dinners kept him involved with the game, but none of it replaced the sheer thrill of playing for Kent or the fellowship of the dressing room.

In 1987 he was offered out of the blue the managing directorship of Kent Indoor Cricket Ltd, a company set up to capitalise on the boom in the indoor game played by two teams of eight a side. Seeing this as a chance to remain in cricket, he hoped that the company would set up four indoor centres in the county within the next few years. Having established one at Becton in east London in November 1987, Underwood began talks with the directors of Gillingham Football Club to open an indoor centre at their Priestfield Stadium sports complex. Although certain reservations were expressed by some councillors that the local community might not get much use of the centre, the leisure service committee gave it its blessing and the centre was opened in April 1989 by Jimmy Hill. Thereafter the business ran into trouble and Underwood left later that year. His brother Keith harboured doubts about its financial viability and the impact it could have on his reputation and Underwood, who was always risk-averse, reached the same conclusion.

He soon found employment with Club Turf Cricket Ltd, pioneers and leading suppliers of artificial cricket pitches worldwide, set up by Keith McGuinness in 1978. Joining as director of cricket, he was a valuable catch given his status in the game and McGuinness was quite happy when Club Turf was referred to as Underwood's company. Concentrating mainly on the south-east and south-west, he visited many clubs and schools advising them what facilities would best suit them. While not proficient at the surveying side (he once did a ground survey from the pavilion when it was raining), he could see the pitfalls, ask the right questions and write neat, concise reports, all of which bore his personal stamp and signature. More important, he was a superb salesman, putting his affable personality and cricketing pedigree to good use. A welcome visitor at independent schools, where his mere presence was normally enough to win the contract, he would often mark the opening of new facilities with either a question-and-answer session or a coaching clinic which invariably went down well.

The volume of work, however, was arduous, not least the travelling – he even ventured as far as Scotland – and because of his fractious relationship with McGuinness it came as a huge relief when he teamed up with his brother.

Returning south in 1983 to work for Abu's parent company which had taken premises in London, Keith Underwood moved to Cheshire in 1989 when the firm relocated there. Parting company with it soon afterwards, he briefly worked for North Western Blanks Ltd in Middleton before taking to the road selling fishing tackle. In 1992 he founded Underwood Agencies, which sold cricket ground equipment to clubs and schools, a move which led to him and his son Kevin becoming sales agents for Club Turf in the north. With McGuinness keen to take a back seat, they purchased the company in 2005, Keith becoming managing director and Kevin operations manager.

Despite Underwood being money-motivated, Kevin recalls him as very good company who opened doors for Club Turf at a time when it was winning large ECB contracts, not least his ability at playing a room and taking an interest in everyone. He came up with the idea of sand-grass in the bowlers' run-ups to protect them from mud and shortening the net roof to make it easier to flight the ball. He did, however, fall short in his total failure to master technology. Leaning incessantly on Kevin to help him work his computer, he would soften him up by saying, 'I'm only a little left-arm tweaker bowler.'

Unlike some of his team-mates such as Boycott, Willis and Knott who never played cricket again once they'd retired, Underwood continued to don his flannels in charity matches for many years. To celebrate Australia's bi-centenary in 1988, he played in three one-day internationals for the England Centenary Test team of 1977 against their Australian counterparts in Australia and in the third game he suffered the indignity of David Hookes hitting him for 23 in one over.

That summer he faced a less formidable opponent when bowling to author and politician Jeffrey Archer in a charity game. Having bowled him first ball he was less than pleased when non-striker Ian Botham called no-ball but, showing little sympathy for his victim, he repeated the treatment again next delivery so that Archer was out for a king pair.

In 1989 he played for the owner of *The Cricketer* Ben Brocklehurst's XI against the Allsorts and was quickly among the wickets until the last-wicket pair held up progress. One short when the game began, the Allsorts gladly recruited Barrie Lloyd, an accomplished club batsman who sneaked off from a lunch party nearby in search of a game. He helped Philip Rudd add 50-odd runs, compelling the opposition to recall Underwood, who promptly had Lloyd caught behind off a lifter by a young Mark Pougatch, later a leading sports broadcaster. As they left the field, Underwood turned to Pougatch and said, 'Alan Knott would have been proud of that catch.' 'I'm sure he was just being very polite,' recalled Pougatch, 'but I didn't care. I went straight home and told my father.'

Later that year Underwood captained an Old Kent XI against an Old Sussex XI to mark the final game ever played at Hastings before that historic ground was turned into a supermarket, a travesty if ever there was one.

In 1990 Underwood was contracted to play for the recently relegated Bankfoot in the Bradford League at £500 per game.

They played 50-over cricket and wanted him to bowl at one end throughout, to which he replied, 'I'm 42 [sic], no way.' In the end he played in half of the 26 games spread over the course of the season. Exposed to some grounds with small boundaries, he was hit for six sixes by Brighouse in the Priestley Cup, the knockout competition of the Bradford League; he also took a pounding against Saltaire, but gradually he regained his former mastery and in his final game he took five wickets against Ben Rhydding to ensure Bankfoot of promotion. Despite finishing top of the Division Two bowling averages, he opted for a gentler form of cricket thereafter although the old competitiveness never entirely disappeared.

In the mid-1990s he made his debut for the 40 Club (open to those of a certain standard beyond the age of 40), captained by his good friend Carl Openshaw, a retired company director who later became chairman of Kent. In his first game against Sevenoaks School, he bowled tidily for a couple of wickets but was somewhat surprised to be hit for six by some young buck as the school chased victory in the final over. He also played against Lancing College before telling Openshaw that he would rather not play again for the club because he couldn't get used to the decrepit fielding.

He represented an Old England XI, participating in two one-day internationals against Old West Indies in Barbados in 1992 and in the BSI World Masters Competition in Bombay in 1995, helping England to reach the semi-final. According to the *Times of India*, his bowling was the difference between victory and defeat for England against Australia. Sunil Gavaskar wrote, 'They used to say of Derek Underwood that even if you woke him from a deep sleep and asked him to bowl, he would pitch the first ball on the spot and he has shown that he has lost none of that ability.'

He played against Old West Indies in Grenada in 2004. Keeping wicket to him, Steven Rhodes thought Underwood, aged 58, bowled better than some county spinners. Not every game was a throwback to the past. John Lever recalls captaining an Old England XI against Loughton Cricket Club in Essex and Underwood being hit about by the Sri Lankan opener. When the South African number three treated him with similar disdain, he said to him, 'Have you got any local players? I can't take this any longer.'

Through his work for Club Turf, Underwood became patron of the newly created Les Ormes Cricket Club, situated in the beautiful grounds of a 16th-century chateau in northern Brittany, and he took a side to play there in 1997.

Club Turf also brought him into contact with Irish cricket in the late 1990s. The Northern Ireland Cricket Association (NCU), founded to foster links between the North and North-West Unions, were recipients of a huge grant from the Sports Council for the installation of artificial pitches at 40 grounds. Club Turf won the contract to install the pitches and Underwood became a frequent visitor. He and Keith McGuinness were the architects of the Club Turf Ulster Cup featuring the top teams in both unions in a 40-over tournament played on artificial pitches.

He invariably attended the final as the competition carried his company's name until 2013 and spoke at many club dinners without a fee, including the 50th anniversary of the Association of Cricket Umpires and Scorers in 1999. Not a natural orator, Underwood spent a lot of time working on his speeches and developed into an accomplished after-dinner speaker, displaying a nice line in humour that was appreciated by his audience.

In 2005 he declined a handsome fee from Channel Four to conduct a leading master class during the England–Australia Test at Old Trafford to honour a commitment to organise an Old England XI to play against an NCU President's XI at Stormont. Not only did his presence draw a healthy attendance – many told him that they'd come to see him – he delighted them by taking three wickets. Later, when president of MCC, he consolidated his ties with Irish cricket by inviting their leading representatives to his box for the England–Australia Test at Lord's.

In 1997 Underwood became patron of the Primary Club, the cricketing charity that provides sports and recreational facilities for the blind and visually impaired. Established in 1955 by four Beckenham cricketers who'd all been dismissed first ball, membership was originally limited to those who played for or against Beckenham; later it was opened to all and sundry after Brian Johnston began to promote it in on *Test Match Special*.

Well qualified to be patron by virtue of getting a king pair in one day playing for Kent against the South Africans in 1965, and six first-ballers in Test cricket, Underwood once participated in a blind game. As he prepared to bowl, he heard the batsman say to his partner, 'It's all right, he can't bowl.' Aside from presiding over a rapid expansion of membership and opening new facilities, he spoke at the first ever Primary Club dinner at the Banqueting Suite, Lord's, in 2003 with fellow speakers Mike Brearley and Mike Brace, chairman of the British Paralympic Association, an occasion which raised over £17,000. Two years later, he spoke at the club's Golden Jubilee at the NatWest Media

Centre, Lord's, with Richie Benaud, patron of the Primary Club of Australia.

He also led the club against the Bunbury Celebrity XI at Ascott Park, Bedford, in 1999, against Beckenham the following year and against the Primary Club of Australia in 2005.

Later that year Underwood played his final game overseas. The previous year Grenada had been devastated by a hurricane, their first for 49 years, which left 45 people dead and 11,000 homeless. As a goodwill gesture, an Old England XI captained by Allan Lamb flew out to the island to donate cricket equipment in schools – the ecstatic reception from the children left wicketkeeper Paul Nixon almost in tears – and to play a Twenty20 against an Old West Indies XI. As a veteran traveller to an island he loved for its climate, food and people, Underwood was delighted to go. Now aged 60, he took a wicket with his first ball, finished with figures of 2-7 and received the largest cheer from the 3,000 crowd as he left the field.

It was through his friend Nick Byers, a director at De Beers UK and member of Antwerp Cricket Club, that Underwood became associated with the latter. Each year he invited him to play in his XI while brother Keith umpired, putting them up in a De Beers apartment in Antwerp.

He became their club president and persuaded former Surrey and England wicketkeeper Jack Richards, who lived in Belgium, to coach the national team. It was against Antwerp that Underwood, now 62, playing for his President's XI, made his final appearance in 2007, bowling club chairman Dennis Newport with a beauty. 'The ball pitched outside leg,' Newport explained. 'I went forward as far as my aching bones could, but it went past the bat and left my off bail lying on the floor. I walked past his brother Keith, who was umpiring, and he said, "That's the best ball he's bowled in ten years."'

From the time of the England tour of Australia in 1986/87 for the next 25 years or so, Underwood acted as a courier for cricket supporters' tours for travel firms such as Gullivers and Standpoint. With his wealth of contacts, natural courtesy and willingness to talk cricket, he was ideal for this role. His good friend John Nye recalls him saying to him in 1986, 'Come to Australia and I'll look after you.' He was as good as his word, introducing him in Perth to the Channel Nine commentary team.

Even when not on official duty he could still strike a good turn that lingered in the memory, as Chris Coke, on a supporters' tour to Jamaica with his wife in 2009, recalls. 'Our birthday arrangements were made for Derek to sit with us for dinner. His unassuming manner, interest in both of us and some tales of his time at Kent made it a very special evening for both of us.'

Following the death of Les Ames in 1990, Underwood succeeded him as controller (president) of the Kent Hoppers Tie Club. The club was formed in a fit of pique by Kent players in May 1939 because the committee had introduced an official club tie that wasn't available to professionals. Indignant that he couldn't purchase a tie for his father who was a member for his birthday, Les Ames and team-mate 'Hopper' Levett, one of Underwood's favourite ex-players, decided to design their own tie bearing its barrels and hops on a dark blue background. At their annual lunch at Canterbury Underwood was his usual genial self, inviting John Major as guest speaker in 2009 and leading to speculation that he might nominate the former Prime Minister as his successor as president of MCC. Instead that honour went to Johnny Barclay.

In 1992 Underwood and Graham Johnson were co-opted to the Kent cricket committee by its chairman Derek Ufton to help bridge the gap between the committee and the players. It was an imaginative move. As a trustee of the Kent Cricket Youth Trust, a charity to support youth cricket, and the president of AKCC for the Metropolitan area, Underwood was a great ambassador visiting schools, handing out prizes and conducting coaching sessions.

On more general matters he contributed little of significance, preferring to stay clear of controversies such as the Canterbury ground's redevelopment plans but was extremely supportive of players such as Matt Walker, Kent's head coach between 2017 and 2024. Never thrusting himself forward or trumpeting his own achievements he willingly helped when asked, especially with left-arm spinner Min Patel, advising him about his field placings and getting him to bowl a shade faster.

Among his family commitments Underwood took prime responsibility for his ailing mother. After living for years in her Keston home, she lost much of her mobility because of a botched knee operation and moved into a nursing home at Sevenoaks, remaining mentally alert until the end. She died in 2006 aged 93.

By 1996 the Underwoods had lived at Sevenoaks for 17 years and now that both girls had completed their education at Combe Bank, an independent girls' day school where they'd excelled at dancing, they were ready for a change. They moved to a salubrious oasthouse at Matfield, an attractive village six miles from Tunbridge Wells. It was there that they hosted the wedding reception of their daughter Heather in July 1998 to the Revd John Hookway, vicar of Christ Church, Ware, following

A peerless cover drive against the West Indies: The Oval 1976.

Underwood with his daughters, Heather and Fiona

Underwood celebrates the regaining of the Ashes with Bob Woolmer and captain Mike Brearley: Headingley 1977.

Graham Gooch leads out the England Rebel tour to South Africa team in 1982, with Peter Willey (left) and Underwood (right).

Underwood, as senior professional, taking the field at Canterbury.

Underwood, as president of MCC, introduces Australia captain Ricky Ponting to Queen Elizabeth II: Lord's 2009.

Underwood with younger daughter Fiona in the President's Box during the England–Australia Test: Lord's 2009.

Underwood, representing his firm Club Turf Ltd, delivers artificial nets to Fettes College: May 1992. On the left is the school professional Jack van Geloven, the former Leicestershire all-rounder who did the double in 1962, and in the middle, Tim Morrison, who donated the nets to the school. Ralph Hughes, Fettes College

Underwood with brother Keith at Kevin Underwood's wedding, 2004.

A dedicated
grandfather to Fiona's
children Oliver [left]
and Alfie [right].

The author
wishes to thank
Mrs Fiona
Simmons and
the Underwood
family for their
help in supplying
many of the
photographs.

Final over. Underwood
with Heather, left, and
Fiona, right.

their marriage at St George's, Weald, the evangelical church where she'd previously worked and worshipped.

One sadness during this time was Underwood's growing detachment from Dawn. Marriage to a top-flight cricketer places a great strain on both parties because of the long absences, especially during the winter. Even when together, there was little escape from the game. 'Cricket has ruled our lives, and an evening hardly goes by when some aspect of cricket is not mentioned,' Dawn wrote in Underwood's 1986 benefit brochure. Accepting the situation for what it was, Dawn focused on her own life bringing up the children, a routine that became rather disrupted when Underwood was home full-time post-retirement. Given their different personalities, life became harder and after a trial separation they decided to split permanently in 2002, a decision which caused little surprise to their friends. Civilities, however, were maintained and they came together for the wedding of Fiona, a qualified dietician, in 2006 to Jamie Simmons, a modern languages teacher in Solihull and avid Wolves supporter. The marriage took place at Wateringbury Church, where Dawn now lived and worshipped, and the reception was held at Paddock Wood Hop Farm.

Needing a firm anchor in his life, Underwood became fully involved with Josie Jones, a New Zealand hotelier, whom he'd first met in Melbourne during the 1977 Centenary Test and whom he continued to see whenever in Australia. (She later managed a hotel in Perth.) A forthright personality who astounded John Woodcock by informing him that she used to serve him his kippers in a Melbourne hotel, she had a keen interest in cricket and she travelled to Britain to manage a hotel at Maidenhead before moving in with him.

In 2006 Underwood was nominated by the outgoing president of Kent, Richard Collins, to be his successor, an ambassadorial role for which he was eminently suited. It was during his final days in office that former team-mate Bob Woolmer, then coach of Pakistan, died of a heart attack in Jamaica, one of the venues for the 2007 World Cup. Shattered by the news, Underwood called him the greatest cricket enthusiast he knew and a brilliant coach.

In 2008 MCC president Mike Brearley asked Underwood, an honorary life member since 1993, to succeed him. 'Why me?' Underwood asked. 'Because I like you,' Brearley replied. Later he expanded on his reasoning. 'He was a distinguished cricketer and has since worked hard within cricket administration. He is a gentle man, conscientious and considerate, but also tough.'

Receiving such an honour from Brearley meant a lot to Underwood and he in turn praised him for helping to 'temper the aloofness and elitism of the MCC'. 'And it changed dramatically, believe me. When I walked through the Long Room in my playing days, I was Underwood. These days I'm Derek. The presidency used to be reserved for the titled gentry, but now it's on a level.'

His presidency coincided with the rise and fall of Sir Allen Stanford, a ruthless American billionaire who signed a deal with the England and Wales Cricket Board (ECB) the previous summer for five Twenty20 games at his personal stadium on the island of Antigua. The final on 1 November, which saw an England XI lose to a West Indies XI by ten wickets, attracted scathing criticism, not least for the inappropriate way in which Stanford treated some of the players' wives. When Stanford was charged with a £5.6 billion investment fraud in the United

States in February 2009, the ECB's reputation was further undermined.

Commenting on the controversy in his presidential role, Underwood wrote, 'Suffice it to say, little has been gained and much might have been lost. On the other hand, the game has always experimented with projects, and in that sense a lesson has been learned.'

Weeks after the Antigua debacle England's tour of India was badly interrupted by the terror attacks in Mumbai (formerly Bombay) leading to the team flying home. While former captains such as David Gower and Mike Atherton called for their return, Underwood was more cautious, highlighting the problems with safety. In the end, after a rescheduled itinerary and heightened security, the team returned to play the two Tests without incident.

Early in 2009 Underwood represented MCC at three Tests in the West Indies, where England were playing, and had the pleasure of meeting Charlie Griffith for the first time since he felled him with a bouncer on his Test debut.

He was also present at the newer cricketing outpost of La Manga, which was hosting its first cricket club tournament in recognition of its work in expanding cricket in Spain. A frequent visitor to the resort since Club Turf installed a couple of pitches there, Underwood enjoyed its climate and hospitality, playing golf with his great friend Rachael Heyhoe Flint, the former England women's cricket captain, who had an apartment there and who did much to establish it as one of Europe's leading sport and leisure centres.

At MCC's annual meeting in May, he reminded members about the importance of the Spirit of Cricket and hoped that, for all the attractions of Twenty20 and the IPL, Test cricket would remain paramount.

He used his time in office to promote youth development in cricket through Chance to Shine, a national charity that partnered with MCC to facilitate the playing of cricket in state schools and rescue the plight of the spinner, something about which he felt strongly. 'The ball is being hit further and further these days, or as the years go by, more and more regulations are being brought in whereby the spinner just isn't getting a decent crack. Is it right that balls going off the splice still fly for six?'

Helped by Josie with her background in corporate hospitality and love of the limelight, Underwood proved the perfect host on matchdays at Lord's. Irish cricket journalist Robin Walsh, one of his guests in the President's Box for the Australia Test, had the pleasure of meeting three of Don Bradman's 1948 Invincibles and when he asked Sam Loxton, a tank commander with the Second Australian Armoured Division in the Second World War, what he thought of batsmen wearing helmets, Loxton replied, 'Helmets, we didn't even wear them at Tobruk!'

Underwood's finest hour came when he entertained the Queen and the Duke of Edinburgh at Lord's for the England–Australia Test, the first time that the Queen had ever had lunch there. Carrying himself with his customary poise, despite his nerves beforehand, he helped create such a relaxed atmosphere that the royal couple clearly enjoyed themselves. Indeed, when it was suggested to the Queen that it was time to leave, she remarked, 'Oh, but I might miss an Australian wicket,' to which Peter Carroll, an MCC committee member who grew up in Sydney, retorted, 'But Ma'am, you are Queen of England and Australia.' The Queen laughed and agreed that he had a point.

Earlier that year Underwood had rung Johnny Barclay, the man whom he'd dismissed for a pair on debut in 1973, and said in his most formal voice, 'John, I would like you to succeed me next year as president of MCC.' 'But Derek, 'I'm not nearly grand enough,' replied the debonair Barclay.

Once his presidential year was over, Underwood's relationship with Josie fizzled out – he wasn't prepared to commit to marriage – and he now took up with Pat Cheesman, a widow who lived close by. The daughter of a Kent builder and avowed cricketer supporter who knew Underwood well, her pleasant, caring nature proved a godsend in his hour of need. She took him to see Keith and Anne in Cheshire where the welcome was as warm as ever and as the discussion turned to cricket, Underwood's personal reminiscences won him a ready audience from his great-nephew Jacob, now a strapping fast bowler of real promise.

He also derived great pleasure from visiting Heather and John, a rugby enthusiast, and their two girls in Ware and Fiona and Jamie and their two boys in Solihull.

He continued to be supportive of various charities, not least the West Kent branch of the Lord's Taverners along with his good friend George Cohen, the Fulham full-back who played in England's World Cup-winning team of 1966, and became a director of Stars Foundation for Cerebral Palsy.

In addition he hosted many charitable golf days primarily at Chart Hills, Biddenden, where he was president. Not a natural golfer with his short swing and handicap of 18, he remained a steely competitor, practising more than he let on. 'If it really mattered you would never beat me,' he said to his good friend Ian Ward.

As president of Matfield, the cricket club where the author Siegfried Sassoon used to play, he helped raise money for a new pavilion after the existing one was severely damaged by fire and he opened it in June 2014 during a game against East India Cricket Club, of whom he was also president.

Having previously had a horse race at Folkestone and a block of flats on the Old Dover Road in Canterbury named after him, in January 2009 he was elected an honorary fellow of Canterbury Christ Church University in a ceremony in Canterbury Cathedral. Then that July he was one of 55 inaugural members inducted into the ICC Hall of Fame when it was launched in 2009. Five years earlier he'd been chosen in England's greatest post-war team unveiled in the October 2004 edition of the *Wisden Cricketer* by a panel of 25, including six former England Test captains. The team in batting order read: Len Hutton (captain), Graham Gooch, Peter May, Denis Compton, Ken Barrington, Ian Botham, Alan Knott, Jim Laker, Fred Trueman, Alec Bedser and Derek Underwood. While Underwood's tally of 297 wickets far exceeded that of his two main rivals, Tony Lock – 174 wickets at 25.6 – and Johnny Wardle, both of whom played in an era when there were fewer Tests, he could count himself fortunate to have been chosen ahead of Wardle. Dogged by a reputation for abrasiveness, which led to MCC cancelling his invitation to tour Australia in 1958/59 after Yorkshire sacked him for publicly criticising the captain, Wardle has never achieved the recognition he merits. An outstanding spinner who could bowl googlies and chinamen as well as slow left-arm orthodox, he took 102 wickets in 28 Tests at an average of 20.39, the lowest average by any recognised spin bowler since the First World War.

In 2010 Underwood was reunited with all the surviving members of the Championship-winning side of 1970 when they congregated at Canterbury for a 40th anniversary dinner. The following year he and Knott, who'd lived in Cyprus since 2002, returned to the St Lawrence Ground in Canterbury Week to open the stand adjacent to the pavilion named in their honour. The precise name caused some debate among the committee. Many thought the mention of the Knott–Underwood Stand wouldn't sound right over the PA in case people thought they'd heard, 'Not the Underwood Stand.' There was also some comment that Underwood should come first, since he'd made his debut for Kent and England before Knott, a view that Underwood, ever the competitor, shared. Their appearance raised the biggest cheer of the day and Knott was pursued by so many autograph hunters that he had to neglect his lunch companions.

That year Underwood was appointed a trustee of MCC and the following year he took part in a question-and-answer session with Tony Greig, who'd given the MCC Spirit of Cricket Cowdrey Lecture, in which he explained the background to WSC and how it had delivered many benefits. When the infamous run-out of Alvin Kallicharran was raised, Greig gave a robust defence of his actions, much to Underwood's amusement. He'd been bowling at the time and recalled how relieved he was that Greig's throw had hit the stumps otherwise it might have gone for four overthrows.

It was a very convivial evening shot through with nostalgia and Underwood much enjoyed being reunited with Greig, a man who'd always raised his spirits. It was to be their last meeting because six months later Greig was dead, three days before the death of Christopher Martin-Jenkins, another of Underwood's good friends. He attended his memorial service at St Paul's Cathedral the following spring and was his vivacious self at the reception afterwards in the Lord's pavilion. When he and Pat met *The Times* journalist Ivo Tennant, Pat asked him, 'How good was Derek?' 'The best,' retorted Tennant, eliciting a gentle smile from Underwood.

Days later Mike Denness passed away, becoming the sixth member of Kent's Championship side – Cowdrey, Luckhurst, Nicholls, Leary and Woolmer – to die. By now Underwood was cutting back on his commitments because of failing health and soon his life was entering the twilight zone.

Chapter 13

'RIP Deadly'

FOR NEARLY 70 years Underwood had enjoyed robust health and hardly ever missed a game because of illness or injury. In retirement he remained fit, giving up smoking, but all that began to change in 2012 when he displayed the first symptoms of Lewy Body Dementia, the second-most common form of dementia, a devastating brain disorder for which there is no cure. Its main symptoms include hallucinations and hearing voices that aren't present, along with problems in movement, concentration and memory. The first signs that something was wrong came when Underwood started seeing lights that weren't there, which put an end to his driving. He became more stressed about money and security and although Turf Cricket tried to keep him on as a consultant, he lacked the necessary energy to continue.

Another early sign of trouble was evident to Keith when, on a trip to Dubai, he noted Underwood's extreme agitation as he kept on asking the whereabouts of the bus they were due to catch, something he'd never witnessed before.

He struggled with a question-and-answer session with Alan Knott and friends detected the loss of memory, the struggle to keep up with conversation and the difficulty of pouring wine into a glass. During the early stages of his condition, Pat was able to drive him to events – he opened the new indoor school at Beckenham with Rob Key in June 2015 – and on one of his final visits to Lord's he had a conversation with Prime Minister Theresa May.

Shortly after receiving his diagnosis Kevin Underwood recalls his uncle letting out his frustration, thinking he'd been unfairly treated and fearful of the future. Although naturally sympathetic of his plight, Kevin reminded him that he'd enjoyed a wonderful life and had plenty of time to put his affairs in order, words that weren't greatly appreciated.

Clive Radley and John Lever used to take him to the cricket at Canterbury, where he would spend some of the time staring into space, but this pleasure came to an end as his condition deteriorated. One close friend last saw him at a Hoppers Club lunch when he clung to him in great distress and wouldn't let go. His final public appearance (in a wheelchair) came at a service at Canterbury Cathedral in March 2020 to celebrate the 150th anniversary of Kent CCC.

By then he'd moved into a care home in Tonbridge, and he soon required 24-hour supervision, which placed an added strain on his finances. Given his condition, close friends such as John Shepherd chose not to visit him, preferring to remember him as they knew him, but he did send him messages on Kent radio, some of which Underwood understood.

In his last years, having survived longer than predicted, he was confined to bed or his chair, attended to sympathetically by Pat but barely able to recognise anyone. On a visit in June 2021 Keith, Anne and Kevin found him with his eyes closed and non-verbal, but when Kevin began chatting to him Underwood opened his eyes and replied with a smile, 'I know that voice.' Later staff told the family that Underwood had experienced his best day for ages.

Over a year later when they visited again, he was completely non-verbal and only Kevin with his loud voice elicited some small recognition. It was the last time that the brothers were to meet.

It was deeply ironic that Keith had also developed dementia and although his condition was less severe than Underwood's, he suffered from other health complications and died in June 2023, aged 81. Perhaps it was a blessing that Underwood remained unaware of the death of a brother whose loyalty and devotion endured to the very end.

Later that year, Kevin, who was working in the area, talked about visiting him but his daughters and Pat advised against it because he'd deteriorated significantly. As he continued to eat less and sleep more, it was clear that the end was near. His death on 15 April 2024 cast a shadow across the cricket world and beyond. The next day flags flew at half-mast across grounds and the Kent team wore black armbands as cricket writers and former team-mates united in tribute to one of England's most revered spinners.

'The Kent Cricket family is in mourning following the passing of one of its greatest ever players,' commented club chairman Simon Philip. 'Derek was an outstanding bowler for both Kent and England, winning trophies for club and country and etching his name in the history books for evermore. Watching Derek weave his unique magic on a wet wicket was a privilege for all who were able to witness it.'

'Derek was one of the greatest bowlers I played with,' wrote Geoff Boycott in the *Daily Telegraph*. 'There has never been anything like him since. He was one of my favourite cricketers.' Vic Marks in *The Guardian* called him a hero from another age. 'A man with a huge heart and no ego.'

To Paul Newman in the *Daily Mail*, 'Underwood was a true gent of the English and world game whose England Test record wickets tally for a spinner may never be beaten.'

The Times' Mike Atherton wrote, 'He was a mild-mannered, friendly and humble man, who radiated charm and gentle humour, but when a wet (unprepared) pitch began to dry, forming a crusty top, he was a destroyer.'

'What a bowler and above all what a lovely guy,' Sunil Gavaskar told *The Times of India*. 'Cricket is poorer with his passing. RIP "Deadly".' It was a message echoed by countless people online as, harking back to that memorable day at the Oval in 1968, they recalled an English sporting legend.

A private funeral for family and close friends – Alan Ealham, Christopher Cowdrey, Richard Ellison, Pat Pocock and John Shepherd among cricketers – was held at the Sussex and Kent Crematorium, Tunbridge Wells on 8 May. Both Heather and Fiona gave eloquent tributes to their father and Christopher Cowdrey talked warmly about the man he had known for 50 years. He also read out an appreciation from Alan Knott who couldn't be present because he was about to receive his 2020 MBE in an investiture postponed due to Covid. Recalling their first encounter at the Eltham nets aged 12 when they were both opening bowlers and Underwood's qualities that 'made him one of the greatest bowlers of all time', Knott concluded: 'From Eltham to forever what a life we had. Deadly, we were all so lucky to have known you and played with you. May your next journey be as great.'

His words not only evoked a glorious era in Kent's history – they also spoke of an exceptional partnership between two remarkable cricketers the like of which we will never see again.

Derek Underwood

One of the great paradoxes of Derek Underwood's career is how such a mild-mannered person should be embroiled in two of cricket's greatest controversies: Kerry Packer's WSC and the England rebel tour of South Africa in 1982.

Born into a loving family and raised in comfortable circumstances, his stable upbringing shaped his conventional outlook. Fully at home in the ordered world of first-class cricket, he conformed to its proprieties by proving a model professional and never speaking out of turn. Yet still waters conceal turbulent currents and Underwood, like many top-class cricketers, chafed at the insensitive treatment accorded them by the game's authorities. Not only were they paid a pittance, especially in comparison to other sportsmen, they were subjected to petty restrictions on tour and ruthlessly disposed of at a whim. (Underwood lost count of the number of times he heard of his omission from the England team on the radio without any explanation.)

Although he was the only player on Ray Illingworth's 1970/71 tour of Australia willing to play in the rearranged Melbourne Test without extra remuneration, money became increasingly important to him after his marriage, making him a potential recruit to Packer's insurgent army. Yet while greatly attracted by the riches on offer, his decision to join proved more troubling than most, given the world he was leaving behind.

An Englishman to his bootlaces, exemplified by his love of playing at festival grounds such as Canterbury and Tunbridge Wells with their idyllic backdrops and genteel ambience, the charge that he deserted his country bit deep. Although adamant that he harboured no regrets about joining WSC, the novelty value of night cricket and competing against the game's elite couldn't compare with the thrill of representing his country.

It said much for his determination that, overcoming the heartbreak of broken friendships, he stayed the course and in time his contention that WSC would benefit the game overall was broadly vindicated, since all players were better remunerated. Although not earning the type of money that top cricketers can now amass, Underwood became a wealthy player in his own right, leaving an estate of £823,000 on his death in 2024, the bulk going to his two daughters, Heather and Fiona, and the remainder going to Pat.

Having stepped out of line over WSC it was easier for Underwood to join the England rebel tour of South Africa. Although their defiance offended progressive opinion and the cricket establishment because of the potential disruption it would cause to the international game, the reaction among fellow professionals was more sympathetic. While the three-year ban ended his England career a tad prematurely, the lasting damage to his reputation was minimal, since the main tenets of the Packer revolution became the norm, and multi-racial South Africa was welcomed back into the fold. As the game continued to become more meritocratic, Underwood's rehabilitation was complete when nominated president of Kent in 2006 and of MCC in 2008.

In a career that lasted 25 years Underwood was a unique phenomenon, an unconventional left-arm spinner who bowled at nearly medium pace. An ardent devotee of the game who revelled in continuous bowling and loathed conceding runs, his style was based on relentless accuracy allied to subtle variations of pace and trajectory. In an age of uncovered pitches his ability to extract prodigious turn and lift on rain-affected ones made him all but unplayable.

Refuting the adage that spinners mature late, Underwood proved an exceptionally wise head on young shoulders from the moment he made his Kent debut against Yorkshire in 1963, aged 17. Capturing 100 wickets in his first season, a feat he was to accomplish ten times overall, he headed the national averages in 1966 with 157 wickets at 13.8 and again in 1967, with 136 at 12.37. When he took his 1,000th wicket at the age of 25, only Wilfred Rhodes and George Lohmann had reached this milestone at a younger age.

Making his Test debut in 1966, he came of age at the Oval in 1968 when he bowled England to a famous victory over Australia with minutes to spare. The following summer he decimated New Zealand at Lord's and the Oval and inflicted further pain on Australia at Headingley in 1972. 'You could argue whether he was a genuine spinner or a medium-pacer but on dusty and damp pitches Underwood was the best I played against,' recalled Greg Chappell. Because of the havoc he wreaked on these pitches, he became the victim of inflated expectations. Having destroyed Australia at Headingley, his six-wicket tally on a perfect batting strip at the Oval in the following Test was deemed something of a failure and a contributing factor to England's five-wicket defeat. According to his detractors he lacked success on firm pitches because of his failure to give the ball enough air. England captain Ray Illingworth often omitted him for Norman Gifford, ironic given that the ICC's belated rankings marked him as the world's leading bowler between 1969 and 1973, the very years when Illingworth was in charge, and those urging him to bowl slower included chairman of selectors Alec Bedser and the *Daily Telegraph*'s E.W. Swanton. Yet despite the pressure, Underwood refused to alter his style, and with good reason, claiming that his record spoke for itself.

As pitches began to improve Underwood lost some of his mystique, especially against West Indies with their abundance of left-handers in their upper order. In 17 Tests against them he only once took five wickets in an innings and finished with an overall bowling average of 43.57 compared to 26.36 against Australia, 27.40 against India and 24.11 against Pakistan. At the same time, he learned the art of adapting his bowling to overseas conditions, never better illustrated than against India in 1976/77 when he out-bowled the fabled Indian spinners Bedi and Chandrasekhar. Further proof of his effectiveness was his dismissal six times of Sunil Gavaskar in that series and 12 times overall in Test cricket. The fact that he also dismissed Greg Chappell on 13 occasions and Doug Walters 12 times says much about his prowess. Had he not lost a couple of his peak years to WSC, or had he played in the era of the Decision Review System, which would have won him many lbw decisions, as it did England off-spinner Graeme Swann between 2008 and 2013, he would doubtless have finished with well over 400 wickets. As it was, his total of 297 remains the highest for an England spinner, and the sixth-highest of any England player, making him England's greatest post-war spinner after Jim Laker.

Underwood's unflagging commitment when representing England never wavered when playing for Kent. One of the promising young thoroughbreds that emerged from their stable in the early 1960s along with Alan Knott, Mike Denness and Brian Luckhurst, they fully absorbed the club ethos of dedicated professionalism and team spirit. Under the benign leadership of Colin Cowdrey, they won the Gillette Cup in 1967; then over the next decade they gained a further ten trophies including the County Championship in 1970, 1977 (shared with Middlesex), and 1978. Had the county not been subjected to endless Test calls their record would have been even more striking, but nevertheless it ranks alongside any county in the modern era.

In a side that lacked penetration in their attack to complement their spectacular batting and fielding, Underwood shouldered a colossal burden, something he did uncomplainingly. During the 1960s on uncovered pitches he was at his most prolific, but those who objected to the help he received from home wickets such as Gillingham and Dover would do well to note his record at Bradford, Hastings and Bournemouth. During the 1970s international commitments and firmer batting surfaces meant that he went for a full decade without taking 100 wickets in a season, but he remained the leading light of Kent's one-day attack, putting a curb on the run rate in mid-innings and picking up many a wicket. It says much for his enduring pedigree that at the age of 39 he recorded his best figures in the JPL (6-12 against Sussex) and in his final year he achieved the best return in the Gillette Cup/NatWest Bank Trophy (8-31 against Scotland). He also disproved the sceptics that the move to uncovered wickets in 1980 would undermine his effectiveness, taking 100 wickets for the tenth time in 1983. Even in his 40s, as age began to catch up with him, few dared take liberties against him. When he retired in 1987 his final statistics stood at 2,465 first-class wickets at 20.28, conceding 2.14 runs an over. On 153 occasions he took five wickets in an innings and on 47 occasions he took ten wickets in a match.

In ODIs he played 24 times for England and took 32 wickets at 22.93. In the Gillette Cup/NatWest Bank Trophy he took 77 wickets in 57 matches at 22.2; in the Benson and Hedges Cup he took 107 wickets in 87 matches at 22.75 and in the John Player League he took 346 wickets in 230 matches at 16.89, heading the national averages in 1971 and in 1973. Had he played in the age of Twenty20 with its rapid acceleration of scoring rates he would have needed to have adapted his bowling, but given the way he coped with the expansion of the one-day game in his own time he would surely have succeeded.

His dedication to his bowling applied as much as to his batting and fielding. A genuine tail-ender with a limited range of shots, he surrendered his wicket dearly. In the pre-helmet age, he displayed raw courage in the way he stood up to the quicks, always trying to get into line, even against the most fearsome of bouncers. Struck in the mouth by Charlie Griffith on his England debut, he absorbed further blows to the body, not least against Dennis Lillee and Jeff Thomson in Australia in 1974/75. A specialist nightwatchman who only once failed to survive until stumps, he viewed the role as an opportunity as much as a challenge, since it allowed him to build an innings on the morrow. Two of his highest Test scores – 43 against Pakistan at the Oval in 1974 and 43 against Australia at Sydney in 1979/80 – came in that position, as were his two highest-ever scores, 80 for Kent against Lancashire in 1969 and his maiden century against Sussex in 1984, perhaps the most memorable moment of his career.

In the field Underwood compensated for his unathletic gait with his safe hands, accurate throw and willingness to fling himself in all directions to save runs.

His legacy as a player was awesome, but what was even more telling was the universal admiration and affection he commanded across the cricket world. Among team-mates he was a genial presence in the dressing room with his self-effacing modesty, his gentle humour and his concern for others. As a debutant he looked up to his elders and learned; as senior professional he dispensed advice and encouragement to younger tyros without blowing his own trumpet. He treated his opponents with respect, never stooping to crude one-upmanship and verbal abuse, a point that Asif made in his 1986 benefit brochure. He wrote, 'Derek Underwood was – and still continues to be – one of the most amiable people I have ever met on and off a cricket field. He always has time for a friendly word and no matter how tense the situation is in the middle Derek can always find it in him to give the opposition an encouraging pat on the back.' He thought it strange that the era that produced Underwood also saw the rise of sledging. Asif continued: 'I think people like Derek totally disproved the theory that in order to be fully competitive you had to psyche yourself into a frame of mind in which you hate your opponent to the extent of being desirous of his blood! That is nonsense. I regard sport as one of the more noble forms of human competitive activity and meanness and hatred could not in any way contribute to excellence in such a form of activity. I am sure that people like Derek Underwood prove my point. If you get 297 Test wickets with a smile and wink here and there, it is good enough for me. Another 50 or 60 odd wickets are hardly worth all that foul-mouthed abuse.'

Asif's paean to a true gentleman – a phrase employed by many of the people I spoke to about Derek Underwood – was endorsed by Vic Marks in his tribute to Underwood in *The Cricketer.* 'There were no airs and graces with Deadly. He would happily talk cricket – and spin bowling – with anyone, often seeking the opinion of others as if they knew better than him (which was ridiculous). Here was the antithesis of the aloof superstar sportsman: he was warm and welcoming, often self-deprecating, always devoid of ego.'

These attributes he carried into retirement with his numerous acts of charity, his hosting of cricket supporters' tours and his encouragement of the game at the grass roots. His presidency of Kent and MCC, a fitting recognition of his legacy to cricket, was conducted with his usual finesse and good cheer.

For someone who'd led such a wholesome life it seemed the cruellest of fates that his final years should be clouded by such a terrible illness. Reduced to a life in the shadows, his death in April 2024 was perhaps a merciful release, but that didn't stop the outpouring of grief for a cricketing icon whose gentle nature showed that the humble and meek really can inherit the earth.

Bibliography

Bailey, Trevor, *The Greatest of My Time* (London: Eyre and Spottiswoode, 1968).

Barclay, John, *Life Beyond the Airing Cupboard* (Bath: Fairfield Books, 2008).

Barclay, John, *Lost in the Long Grass* (Bath: Fairfield Books, 2013).

Bartlett, Kit and Crofton, Philip, *Derek Underwood: His Record Innings-by-Innings* (Nottingham: ACS Publications, 2004).

Bedser, Alec, *Twin Ambitions* (London: Collins Willow, 1984).

Blofeld, Henry, *My A-Z of Cricket* (London: Hodder and Stoughton, 2019).

Blofeld, Henry, *The Packer Affair* (London: Collins, 1978).

Botham, Ian, *Century: My 100 Great Cricketing Characters* (London: CollinsWillow, 2002).

Botham, Ian, *The Autobiography* (London: Ebury Press, 2007).

Brearley, Mike, *The Art of Captaincy* (London: Hodder and Stoughton, 1985).

Brearley, Mike and Doust, Dudley, *The Ashes Retained* (London: Hodder and Stoughton, 1979).

Brearley, Mike and Doust, Dudley, *The Return of the Ashes* (London: Pelham, 1978).

Briggs, Paddy, *John Shepherd: The Loyal Cavalier* (Cardiff: ACS Publications, 2009).

Chalke, Stephen, *Caught in the Memory: County Cricket in the 1960s* (Bath: Fairfield Books, 1999).

Chalke, Stephen, *In Sunshine and Shadow: The Biography of Geoff Cope* (Bath: Fairfield Books, 2017).

Chalke, Stephen, *Micky Stewart and the Changing Face of Cricket* (Bath: Fairfield Books, 2011).

Chalke, Stephen, *Summer's Crown: The Story of Cricket's County Championship* (Bath: Fairfield Books, 2015).

Chalke, Stephen, *Tom Cartwright – The Flame Still Burns* (Bath: Fairfield Books, 2007).

Corbett, Ted, *Cricket on the Run* (London: Stanley Paul, 1988).

Cowdrey, Christopher and Smith, Jonathan, *Good Enough?* (London: Pelham, 1986).

Cowdrey, Colin, *MCC: Autobiography of a Cricketer* (London: Hodder and Stoughton, 1976).

Denness, Mike, *I Declare* (London: Arthur Barker, 1977).

Dexter, Ted, *85 Not Out* (Shrewsbury: Quiller, 2020).

D'Oliveira, Basil, *An Autobiography* (London: Collins, 1968).

D'Oliveira, Basil, *Time to Declare* (London: J.M.Dent, 1980).

Ellis, Clive and Pennell, Mark, *Trophies and Tribulations: 40 Years of Kent Cricket* (London: Greenwich Publishing, 2010).

Frindall, Bill, *Bearders: My Life in Cricket* (London: Orion, 2006).

Frith, David, *Silence of the Heart* (Edinburgh: Mainstream, 2001).

Frith, David, *The Slow Men* (London: Allen and Unwin, 1984).

Gatting, Mike, *Leading from the Front* (London: Queen Anne Press/Fontana, 1988).

Gavaskar, Sunil, *Idols* (London: Allen and Unwin, 1983).

Gooch, Graham and Lee, Alan, *Out of the Wilderness* (London: Grafton, 1986).

Graveney, Tom, *Cricket over Forty* (London: Pelham Books, 1970).

Greig, Tony, *My Story* (London: Stanley Paul, 1980).

Griffith, Charlie, *Chucked Around* (London: Pelham, 1970).

Haigh, Gideon, *The Cricket War: The Story of Kerry Packer's World Series Cricket* (London: Wisden, 2017).

Hill, Alan, *Les Ames* (London: Christopher Helm, 1990).

Illingworth, Ray, *Spin Bowling* (London: Pelham, 1979).

Johnston, Brian, *It's Been a Piece of Cake* (London: Methuen, 1985).

Kelly, Rob, *Hobbsy: A Life in Cricket* (Brighton: Von Krumm Publishing, 2018).

Knott, Alan, *It's Knott Cricket* (London: Macmillan, 1985).

Knott, Alan, *Stumper's View* (London: Stanley Paul, 1972).

Lee, Alan, *A Pitch in Both Camps* (London: Stanley Paul, 1979).

Lewis, Tony, *Playing Days* (London: Stanley Paul, 1985).

Lloyd, Clive, *Living for Cricket* (London: Stanley Paul, 1980).

Lloyd, David, *Simply the Best* (London: Simon and Schuster, 2020).

McGregor, Adrian, *Greg Chappell* (London: Collins, 1985).

McKinstry, Leo, *Boycs: The True Story* (London: Collins Willow, 2000).

Marks, Vic, *Late Cuts: Musings on Cricket* (London: Allen and Unwin, 2022).

Martin-Jenkins, Christopher, *Assault on the Ashes: MCC in Australia and New Zealand 1974–75* (London: MacDonald and Company, 1975).

Martin-Jenkins, Christopher, *Cricket Contest: The Post-Packer Tests* (London: Queen Anne Press, 1980).

Martin-Jenkins, Christopher, *MCC in India 1976–77* (London: MacDonald and Jane's, 1977).

Martin-Jenkins, Christopher, *The Jubilee Tests* (London: MacDonald and Jane's, 1977).

Martin-Jenkins, Christopher, *Testing Time: MCC in West Indies 1974* (London: MacDonald and Jane's, 1974).

Moore, Dudley, *The History of Kent CCC* (London: Guild Publishing, 1988).

Murtagh, Andrew, *Sundial in the Shade: The Story of Barry Richards* (Durrington, Pitch Publishing, 2015).

Murtagh, Andrew, *Test of Character: The Story of John Holder* (Worthing: Pitch Publishing, 2016).

Nicholas, Mark, *A Beautiful Game* (Sydney: Allen and Unwin, 2016).

Peel, Mark, *Cricketing Caesar: A Biography of Mike Brearley* (Worthing: Pitch Publishing, 2020).

Peel, Mark, *The Last Roman: A Biography of Colin Cowdrey* (London: Andre Deustch, 1999).

Peel, Mark, *Yorkshire Grit: The Biography of Ray Illingworth* (Worthing: Pitch Publishing, 2023).

Pocock, Pat, *Percy* (London: Clifford Frost Publications, 1987).

Procter, Mike, *Caught in the Middle: The Autobiography of Mike Procter* (Worthing: Pitch Publishing, 2017).

Richards, Viv, *Sir Vivian: The Definitive Biography* (London: Michael Joseph, 2000).

Roebuck, Peter, *It Never Rains: A Cricketer's Lot* (London: Allen and Unwin, 1984).

Sandford, Christopher, *Laker and Lock: The Story of Cricket's Spin Twins* (Worthing: Pitch Publishing, 2022).

Simpson, Bobby, *The Australians in England 1968* (London: Stanley Paul, 1968).

Snow, John, *Cricket Rebel* (London: Hamlyn, 1976).

Sobers, Gary, *King Cricket* (London: Pelham Books, 1967).

Sobers, Gary, *My Autobiography* (London: Headline, 2002).

Sobers, Gary, *Twenty Years at the Top* (London: Macmillan, 1988).

Stackpole, Keith, *Not Just for Openers* (Abbotsford: Stockwell Press, 1974).

Taylor, Bob, *Standing Up, Standing Back* (London: Collins Willow, 1985).

Tennant, Ivo, *The Cowdreys: Portrait of a Family* (London: Sinclair Stevenson, 1990).

Tossell, David, *Grovel! The Story and Legacy of the Summer of 1976* (Worthing: Pitch Publishing, 2012).

Tossell, David, *Tony Greig: A Reappraisal of English Cricket's Most Controversial Captain* (Worthing: Pitch Publishing, 2011).

Underwood, Derek, *Beating the Bat* (London: Stanley Paul, 1975).

Underwood, Derek, *Deadly Down Under* (London: Arthur Barker, 1980).

Walters, Doug, *Looking for Runs* (London: Pelham Books, 1971).

Ward, Kirwan, *Put Lock On!* (London: Hale, 1972).

West, Peter, *Flannelled Fool and Muddied Oaf* (London: W.H.Allen, 1986).

Whitington, R.S., *Captains Outrageous? Cricket in the Seventies* (London: Stanley Paul, 1973).

Wilkins, Brian, *The Bowler's Art* (London: A & C Black, 1991).

Willis, Bob, *Lasting the Pace* (London: Collins, 1985).

Woolmer, Bob, *Pirate and Rebel? An Autobiography* (London: Arthur Barker, 1984).

Newspapers and Periodicals

Canberra Times, Cricket Paper, Cricketer, Daily Express, Daily Mail, Daily Mirror, Daily Telegraph, East Kent Gazette, Financial Times, Guardian, Hindu, Independent, Kent CCC Annual, Kent, Kent Herald, Kent Messenger, Kentish Advertiser, Kentish Express, Maidstone Telegraph, MCC Newsletter, Observer, Sevenoaks Advertiser, Sun, Sunday Express, Sunday People, Sunday Telegraph, Sunday Times, Thanet Times, Times, Times of India, Tonbridge Free Press, Wisden Cricket Monthly, Wisden Cricketers' Almanack.

Online Resources

ESPN Cricinfo; Wikipedia; www.cricbuzz.com; www.Kentcricket.co.uk, www.thecricketmonthly.com

Acknowledgements

I'D LIKE to thank the following for sharing their experiences of Derek Underwood: Frank Ames, Dennis Amiss, Asif Iqbal, Mark Baker-White, Johnny Barclay, Jack Birkenshaw, Henry Blofeld, Mike Brearley, Stephen Brenkley, Alan Brown, Rodney Cavalier, Chris Coke, Geoff Cope, Christopher Cowdrey, Alan Dixon, Andrew Dixon, Paul Downton, John Dye, Barry Dudleston, Alan Ealham, Richard Ellison, John Emburey, Farokh Engineer, Keith Fletcher, Norman Graham, Mike Griffith, Simon Hinks, Richard Hutton, Graham Johnson, Chris Larlham, John Lever, Steve Marsh, John Nye, Carl Openshaw, Erica Patterson, Pat Pocock, Clive Radley, Mike Selvey, Kevin Sharp, John Shepherd, Jack Simmons, Paul Smallwood, Neil Taylor, Ivo Tennant, Ian Ward, Martin Wigram and Bob Wilson.

In particular, I'd like to thank Mrs Dawn Underwood, Derek's ex-wife, Mrs Anne Underwood, his sister-in-law, and Kevin Underwood, his nephew. Also Derek's daughter, Mrs Fiona Simmons, for her help in supplying family photographs.

I'm grateful to Neil Robinson, the Curator of Collections at Lord's and MCC, and Alan Rees, the Archive and Library Manager at Lord's, for all their efforts on my behalf.

ACKNOWLEDGEMENTS

I am greatly indebted to Ian Phipps, the Heritage Officer at Kent CCC, for all his help in providing me with minutes of the Kent committee and answering any number of inquiries.

I would also like to acknowledge all the help I had from the staff at the National Library of Scotland.

Finally, I'd like to thank Bruce Talbot for his copy edit, and to Jane Camillin and Alex Daley at Pitch, along with Duncan Olner, Dean Rockett and Graham Hales for all their efforts on the design, proofing and typesetting.

Index